RELATIONSHIPS IN RECOVERY

RELATIONSHIPS IN RECOVERY

Healing Strategies for Couples and Families

Emily Marlin

Produced by The Philip Lief Group, Inc.

PERENNIAL LIBRARY

HARPER & ROW, PUBLISHERS • NEW YORK
Grand Rapids, Philadelphia, St. Louis, San Francisco
London, Singapore, Sydney, Tokyo, Toronto

Grateful acknowledgment is made to the following for permission to quote from copyrighted material:

Excerpt from *Making Peace with Food,* by Susan Kano, Copyright © 1989 by the author. Reprinted by permission of Harper & Row, Publishers, Inc.

"The Twelve Steps." Reprinted with permission of Alcoholics Anonymous World Services, Inc.

FIRST EDITION

Designed by Helene Berinsky

Library of Congress Cataloging-in-Publication Data

Marlin, Emily.
  Relationships in recovery: healing strategies for couples and families/Emily Marlin; produced by The Philip Lief Group, Inc.—1st ed.
    p. cm.
  ISBN 0-06-055185-2
  ISBN 0-06-096436-7 (pbk.)
  1. Alcoholics—United States—Family relationships. 2. Alcoholism—Psychological aspects. 3. Alcoholics—Rehabilitation—United States. 4. Codependence (Psychology)—United States. I. Philip Lief Group. II. Title.
HV5132.M347 1990
362.29'23'0973—dc20   89-45687

---

90 91 92 93 94   DT/MP   10 9 8 7 6 5 4 3 2 1
90 91 92 93 94   DT/MP   10 9 8 7 6 5 4 3 2 1 (pbk.)

In Memory of Emily Worthington Marlin
1912–89

CONTENTS

PART III: THE MUTUAL-PARTNER STAGE

ACKNOWLEDGMENTS

Although the process of writing a book can sometimes be isolating, my experience with *Relationships in Recovery* was anything but. Certainly, I spent many long hours at the typewriter and even more hours thinking about the book, but I did not feel all that alone. I knew that other people were involved in the process also. And, most of the time, they were only a quick phone call away.

It was reassuring to have the same encouraging people in my "support system" as I had for my book *Hope: New Choices and Recovery Strategies for Adult Children of Alcoholics* a few years ago. Once again, these people provided the nurturance, nudging, and nagging I needed to keep me moving forward.

The stars of my constellation include the following:

My book packager, The Philip Lief Group, which was enthusiastic about the book from the time it was just an idea; Kevin Osborn, my editor, with whom I had a terrific working relationship and to whom I am grateful for all his suggestions and sensitivities; and Bob Markel, my long-time agent, who is my strongest advocate and smartest adviser (and I think Bob must have felt, on more than one occasion, that he was also my therapist), whose wisdom and guidance were always calming and comforting.

I feel quite lucky to have had the same supportive and knowledgeable person, Janet Goldstein, who was my editor at Harper & Row for the second time, again working on my book. Janet has the greatest respect for her authors, as well as a keen understanding of the material and the market. It is very comforting to know that a book becomes much better in the hands of a skilled editor. I wish to thank my friend Charlotte Henshaw for being not only an excellent and reliable research assistant but my guardian angel/alter ego. Charlotte was emotionally, if not physically, present throughout the entire process and always knew how to keep me centered and the book project organized.

The unidentified heroes and heroines of *Relationships in Recovery* are the men and women I have worked with in my professional practice. To honor confidentiality, I have changed their names and other details to protect their identities. However, I have tried to keep their words as implicitly intact as possible. Their stories are the testaments of the miracle of healing relationships through hard work, commitment, and love. They are powerful examples of how people struggle to sustain and restore themselves and all their personal relationships. They prove that you can find love and happiness in recovery.

RELATIONSHIPS IN RECOVERY

THE ROAD TO RELATIONSHIP RECOVERY

Just by picking up this book, you have revealed your optimism —your hope that things can change for the better. Like everyone else who is reading this book—not to mention all therapists, their patients, and members of self-help groups—you believe, and rightfully so, that your life can improve. As you read this book, I hope you will draw from it the encouragement and guidance you need to make your relationship work. You'll see that the process of recovery is a possible and worthwhile journey.

WHY ISN'T EVERYTHING BETTER YET?

If you have acknowledged the alcoholic's disease and its destructive impact on you, you have already taken an enormous step toward individual recovery and the improvement of your relationship. Even after you have admitted the problem of alcoholism and have begun to recognize its damaging effects on everyone who loves the alcoholic, you will still need to make

1

an effort to overcome the effects of the illness—and any other difficulties in your relationship. Stopping the drinking or changing the way you respond to it is only the first of many steps on the road to recovery. It's a critical step, though, since without it, any further steps taken would head both you and your partner in the wrong direction. But you must go beyond that step to see any marked progress on the road to recovery. *Relationships in Recovery* offers you strategies and advice that will help you move beyond this first step and will lead you toward self-improvement and the recovery of your relationship.

Like most people who are new to recovery, you may have hoped that as soon as both of you committed yourselves to recovery, your interaction would suddenly magically change. Indeed, you may even experience a brief "honeymoon" period —even if you're in a familial relationship or a friendship rather than in a romance. Despite the heady rush of this early period of recovery, this kind of honeymoon quickly ends. Sooner or later, the initial feelings of relief, joy, and boundless hope that mark the honeymoon period give way to a rush of long-forgotten emotions about alcoholism and the alcoholic: sadness, anger, and resentments that you may not have admitted before, even to yourself.

"My father has been sober for two months now, and it's definitely a 'miracle,' no doubt about that," admits Joni, a thirty-eight-year-old office manager. "But I feel very uncomfortable with his changing personality. He's really a very different person, and I guess I don't trust that it will last.

"I keep waiting for him to revert to being the bully he's been for the past seventy years. I feel like a missile is about to blast off and I'll be the target, but I don't know where or when. I guess I just don't trust that this is really going to work. He seems like a pussycat now, but I still see him as that old tiger, ready to strike. So I keep putting myself in the same old defensive position.

"I think I'm also frustrated because he's obviously changing, and I still feel stuck. I don't see that I'm changing. I'm still so guarded. Once he stopped drinking, I expected everything would be fine, that we'd finally be a 'happy family.' But now, here I am feeling very unhappy; I'm resentful and frustrated. I guess I have to change, too, and I really don't want to do that. It's almost like I experience it as a demand. He changed; therefore, we *must*. It makes me mad."

Joni's feelings are typical of those of family members, friends, and lovers who are confronted with an alcoholic's new sobriety. Like Joni, you may be bewildered by the flood of your emotional ups and downs—not to mention the recovering alcoholic's. Moments of doubt, fear, and anger may rush in directly on the heels of hope and exhilaration. Feelings like these are perfectly normal, especially after the long devastation of alcoholism. Like Joni, who spent thirty-eight years living with her father's alcoholism, you may have ample cause to feel angry, uncertain, and distrustful. As the progressive disease of alcoholism accelerates, gaining more and more destructive power, the accumulation of myths, lies, deceits, broken promises, and dashed dreams shatters mutual trust, making loving, intimate relationships impossible. After so many years, you may have grown so accustomed to the alcoholic's pattern of deceit that you don't trust the strange new ways that come with sobriety. Long after the alcoholic in your life has begun to pursue sobriety, your anger, resentment, or distrust may cause you to resist some of the changes it brings to your relationship—*even if you're in recovery yourself!*

"When my wife was drinking, I always knew what to expect," confides Tommy, a forty-year-old firefighter whose wife stopped drinking only six weeks ago. "Social situations were always pretty much the same—a disaster. She would create a big scene, especially if we were in a public place. No matter what restaurant we would go to, she'd complain. The food was lousy, the service terrible. She'd make it miserable for everyone. After a while, we just stopped going out altogether.

"Now that she's sober, I don't know what to expect anymore. Last week we went out to dinner to celebrate our son's eighteenth birthday. I kept expecting the worst, waiting for her to start bitching and moaning. But she never did. Actually, the evening was quite calm. But I wasn't. I couldn't really relax and enjoy the evening. I just kept waiting for her to be miserable and make it miserable for the rest of us."

As you will see in Chapter 7, you can take steps to restore mutual trust by initiating more open and honest communication with each other. But this process takes time and effort. Understandably, Tommy cannot yet trust his wife's sobriety. He will need to experience many more calm evenings out before he can really believe that the absence of alcohol will make a big difference in his wife's behavior. He has expected the worst for so long that he really cannot yet allow himself to expect that things will be much better. His wife has not had a drink in six weeks. That's a fact. But all the previous episodes of alcoholic behavior are facts, too. And it will take a while for Tommy's emotions and reactions to adjust to the new fact of his wife's sobriety.

WHERE WILL RECOVERY TAKE YOU?

You probably have little idea about where recovery will take you and your relationships. You may not be sure what sobriety is, how recovery works, and what these changes can offer you. Certainly you know what you are moving away from, but what are you going toward? Because you will not always be able to answer this question clearly, you may find the beginning of recovery a confusing and even discouraging time. With every new moment, you may wonder what will happen next.

This kind of uncertainty is not only normal, but appropriate. Generally, the beginning of recovery is a confounding time, not just for the person who is newly sober from alcohol, drugs, or some other addictive behavior, but for relatives and close friends, too. No matter what sort of mini-education about alcoholism you may have acquired through counseling, reading, support groups, or rehabilitation centers, nothing can fully prepare you for the enormous changes wrought by recovery. No one, including the recovering addict, really knows what to expect when he or she stops using alcohol or drugs or exhibiting compulsive behavior. Because each individual recovery is unpredictable, it can be just as baffling as addiction itself. It opens up a new territory—unfathomable and unexpected.

In the face of the great unknown, you may have many questions. Wondering what effect the alcoholic's sobriety and your personal recovery will have on your relationships, you may ask yourself:

- In what direction will these changes lead?
- What will happen to my relationship as I change and—I hope—as the alcoholic changes?
- Will my relationship get better or worse?
- Will it end for good or will I be able to make a fresh start?
- Can I find love in my current relationship after recovery?

Since every individual and every relationship follows a unique path of recovery, no one can answer these questions in advance. If you have a general idea of the direction of recovery, however, you can keep the improvement of your relationships on course and give your relationships the best possible chance to survive and flourish. *Relationships in Recovery,* which covers the three major stages of personal and relationship recovery, will, it is hoped, ease some of the confusion and discouragement you may feel along the way. Through suggestions and advice gleaned from my personal and professional experience, I describe some of the predicaments that may lie ahead and ways to resolve them. By using *Relationships in Recovery* to help anticipate and handle some of the problems that may arise in your recovering relationship, you can minimize the impact of these difficulties, which will allow you to stay on track as you move toward self-improvement and the improvement of your relationships.

You can elicit helpful advice from many other guides. Although no one can travel the road to personal recovery or relationship recovery for you, in self-help groups like Al-Anon and in group therapy you will find people who have already experienced many of the difficulties of recovery. Because these people have been in similar situations before, they may be able to offer support and suggestions that will help you stay on the right path toward recovery. Professional therapists, by drawing on their psychological expertise, can also help you handle the unique difficulties of recovery. By reading this book and calling on these and other people for assistance whenever you need it, you will find your own way to better relationships.

STOP, LOOK, AND LISTEN

If you have just started trying to improve your relationship with a recovering alcoholic or addict, you will find it helpful to observe three important guidelines: Stop, Look, and Listen. If you each make a commitment to try to follow these three rules, you will safely cross over to a new way of life in your relationship.

Stop. What is most important is that you will need to stop behaving in the same old ways that characterize alcoholic relationships. Whether or not the alcoholic stops drinking, you and others who are around the alcoholic need to stop letting the alcoholic's actions determine the way you behave. You need to be willing to discontinue shielding the alcoholic from accountability and thus unwittingly allowing the disease to progress. As you recover, you will no longer respond to the alcoholic in the same old destructive way. And by stopping the old ways of behavior and breaking away from the obsolete rules that governed your relationship in illness, you will lay the groundwork for the next stage of relationship recovery.

Look. The center of your attention has to change if you want to change. Each of you needs to break away from the tunnel vision that characterizes addictive relationships: the alcoholic's concentration solely on the next drink and family members' or friends' focus only on the alcoholic's actions. Instead, take some time to look at yourself. Examine the part you played in maintaining the situation or in manipulating it in the hopes that it would disappear. Evaluate what you can and cannot change and appreciate the difference. Change what you can (that is, yourself) and let the rest be.

Listen. To make significant strides forward in your relationship, listen to your own inner voice and to the voices of others. Heed your inner voice when it reminds you of your many personal strengths and your right to get help from others. Whenever you face an important choice about the direction in which to take your relationships, listen to your instincts. Listen to the wisdom of others—friends, professionals, members of Al-Anon or Alcoholics Anonymous (AA), books like this one —which can teach you about the disease of alcoholism and its effect on those touched by it and sometimes suggest routes toward personal or relationship recovery. Most important, listen to your partner as you honestly share what you want from each other and from the relationship you are continuing to build. Listen to the alcoholic whenever he or she tells you that you're asking for something he or she cannot provide.

Relationships in Recovery suggests ways in which you can stop, look, and listen so you may advance your personal recovery and improve your relationships. Although each of these three actions is important in every phase of recovery, each helps define a particular stage of recovery.

THE THREE STAGES OF RELATIONSHIP RECOVERY

In working with couples and families in recovery from alcoholism and other addictions, I have defined three stages that all individuals must move through to improve their relationships. This book guides you through these three stages, which I call the Eye-Opener, the Pioneer, and the Mutual Partner. Identification with these stages can help you pinpoint where you are now in recovery, where you once were, and where you are going. Recognizing the particular stage of recovery that best characterizes you and your relationship will help you confront the unique challenges you need to meet to move through that stage.

As you read about these stages of relationship recovery, you will probably identify with one of them more closely than with the others. In reviewing the characteristics of each stage, note which ones apply to you at this time. If you strongly identify with at least five in any one stage, that's probably the stage you most need to work on.

EYE-OPENERS

- have decided to *stop* the old, self-destructive ways of thinking and behaving that got in the way of relationships;
- have chosen Al-Anon, individual or group therapy, or a combination of the three as a program for individual recovery;
- sometimes still deny the disease of alcoholism and its effects on everyone close to the alcoholic;
- no longer want to pretend that there isn't a problem;
- don't talk much;
- don't trust at all;
- are beginning to recognize inner feelings—positive and negative;
- feel confused much of the time;
- feel angry much of the time;
- sometimes feel ambivalent about the recovery process.

PIONEERS

- have decided to *look* at themselves and pinpoint the qualities they already like and those that need improvement;
- continue to work on getting better through the help of their recovery programs;
- are working hard to discover and establish their identities;
- are developing a deeper understanding of alcoholism and its effect on friends and family members;

- wonder whether they have become too close or too distant from the other people in their lives;
- often feel lonely and afraid;
- make mistakes, but feel okay about them;
- are learning to accept themselves and others;
- try to share their feelings with other people;
- persevere courageously.

MUTUAL PARTNERS

- try to *listen* carefully to their own instincts, as well as to the voices of the alcoholic and others;
- have internalized many lessons from their individual recovery programs;
- continue to change all the time;
- honestly and openly trust, talk, and feel;
- take action to try to resolve conflicts;
- take risks and make decisions;
- freely admit mistakes;
- don't blame themselves or others;
- have established a healthy balance between closeness and distance from other people;
- are bound to others through commitment, common goals, and communication;
- enjoy themselves, their sex lives, and their sobriety.

If you have begun the process of recovery, you can probably place yourself in one of these stages. By using the three stages of relationship recovery as a road map, you can mark your progress toward relationships in recovery. Keep in mind that none of these stages is rigid. Sometimes the stages overlap, so that during certain periods of your recovery you may find yourself "between stages"—exhibiting traits and coping with the challenges of more than one stage. If you do, try to deal with the tasks of the earlier stage first before moving on to the next stage. Each challenge you meet successfully will make the next one that much easier to handle.

As you proceed, try not to rush yourself through the first

two stages in your hurry to become a Mutual Partner. In fact, even if you already see yourself as a Pioneer or a Mutual Partner, take the time to read about the earlier stages. You may read about an issue in an earlier stage that you never fully addressed before. Even more important, by reading about earlier periods of your recovery, you will clearly see how far you have already progressed. And doing so can motivate you to continue your personal and relationship growth.

Everyone follows an individual timetable for recovery, moving through these stages at his or her own pace. One person may stay in the Eye-Opener stage for three months, while another may need to work through that stage for a year. You may feel frustrated when you don't progress as quickly as you would like. You may feel even more frustrated when you experience a small setback in your recovery, for example, when you think you have already "graduated" from a particular stage and you suffer an "emotional slip" that temporarily drops you back to that stage. Try not to give in to impatience and frustration when these things happen (because they certainly *will* happen). Remember that progress never follows a straight line. If you take three steps forward and then one step back, you have still made progress.

THE PROMISE OF RECOVERY

As you embark on the new and mysterious journey called recovery, try not to expect that you will arrive in some wonderful fantasyland, where you will live "happily ever after." Recovery cannot promise eternal bliss. At times, distress and despair will certainly overcome you. During particularly rough moments, you may even feel you are getting worse instead of better. But if you work at recovery, you *will* get better. If you have the courage to confront yourself and your relationships, you have everything you need to explore the uncharted territory of recovery. Gradually, day by day, you will begin to see some improvement in yourself, and as you get better, your relationships will become stronger. In time, you will progress through the three stages of relationship recovery and achieve the satisfaction of having Mutual Partnerships in *all* your relationships.

PART I

The Eye-Opener Stage

PUTTING THE PAST BEHIND YOU

Recognizing and Resisting Codependency

NO MORE DENIAL

If you are in the Eye-Opener stage of recovery, you have decided to stop pretending. After years of hiding from the truth, you want to take charge of your own life and stay in reality. Like most Eye-Openers, you have probably moved beyond major denial—the hallmark of the disease in both addicts and family members. You now accept the fact that alcoholism is a family illness and that you played a part in the disease process. You no longer believe that alcoholism was a problem solely for the alcoholic and realize that it was also a problem for you. Eye-Openers have to stop being part of this problem and instead become part of the solution.

But even when you believe you have moved beyond *major* denial, what I call *minor* denial continues to exert a strong pull. Denial of reality comes in many different sizes and shapes. So even though you've accepted the major reality of the disease, you will need to guard against buying into other minor denials of reality. If you want to maintain your course of recovery, you will need to keep your eyes open for these minor denials.

One common example of a minor denial is the attitude, "I can handle this problem alone." Although they sometimes try, Eye-Openers rarely recover on their own. When households are in the grip of alcoholism, family members often try to employ the strategy of handling things alone. But this kind of thinking never works—either in alcoholism or in recovery.

"Early in my husband's recovery, I felt very alone. He had AA and lots of new friends, but I didn't want to go to Al-Anon. I'd been a few times and thought it wasn't for me," explains Kitty, a thirty-two-year-old waitress whose husband got into a recovery program for his alcoholism a full year before she sought help for herself.

"With him going to all those AA meetings, I felt just as alone as I had when he was out drinking all night, every night. And I felt even worse because I felt guilty for feeling the way I did. I really wanted nothing more than for him to stay sober, but I felt terribly angry, too. It seemed like I was still second best. I had nothing to do and no one to do it with.

"Finally, the pain of my isolation became so incredible that I couldn't stand it anymore. I was angry and depressed all the time. I saw it was my problem and I needed help. I still wasn't ready for Al-Anon, but I started seeing a therapist. She was very understanding and supportive, and she helped me see how my isolation was a big part of my problem.

"After a few months, though, my depression seemed to be getting even worse. 'Now you have to go to Al-Anon,' she told me. I guess I was finally ready, so I just went because she made me go. Things really started to change then. It was amazing how much better I started to feel. I wasn't alone anymore. I had the help I'd resisted for so long, and it was a great relief."

Kitty had spent ten years thinking she could handle her husband's alcoholism—and all the rest of their problems—by herself. Even after admitting her powerlessness over alcoholism, she continued to hold on to the rest of this belief. Kitty's minor denial kept her out of recovery for over a year after her husband had stopped drinking. But once she openly admitted that she couldn't handle everything alone and no longer wanted to do it alone, her recovery started to gain momentum.

If you have just begun your recovery from alcoholism—your own or a loved one's—you will need to work hard just to keep your eyes open to reality. You may have accepted the truth of alcoholism—or even its effects on you—but perhaps you still engage in minor denials of other problems that may be damaging you or your relationships.

Some of the most common of these minor denials include:

- "It's the alcoholic's problem, not mine."
- "Alcoholism is the only problem. Once the alcoholic takes care of it, everything will be fine."
- "The alcoholic's drinking was a serious problem. Fortunately, though, I never lost control of the situation."
- "Alcoholism may have damaged my relationship with the alcoholic, but it hasn't affected any of my other relationships."
- "I'm glad the alcoholic's drinking never affected the kids."
- "The alcoholic's drinking never hurt me."
- "I'm not at all angry about the alcoholic's drinking—and I never was."
- "We don't have any trouble communicating in our relationship."
- "We've always been honest with each other."

As an Eye-Opener, you will need to correct these minor denials. The problems these denials ignore may interfere with the improvement of your life and your relationships. Keep in mind that any denial of reality, no matter how large or small, gets in the way of both individual and relationship recovery. So make a commitment, even if it sometimes seems painful, to stay in touch with reality.

FACING CODEPENDENCY

If you've picked up this book, you have undoubtedly read or heard the word "codependency," and you may already have a pretty good idea of how codependency has fit into your life and relationships. Whatever the particular addiction may be, addicts and those who closely share their lives become overly dependent. Feeling insecure, inadequate, and afraid of emotions, addicts and codependents are both extremely needy. And they come to depend totally on each other to meet their complementary needs. One person—usually the alcoholic—pleads, "I Need You" or "Save Me," and the other person chimes in just as eagerly, "You Need Me" or "I'll Save You." This type of excessively dependent behavior is often called *codependency*.

Codependents devote so much energy to caring for alcoholics that they have no energy left for themselves. As Loretta, one of my patients, described it, codependency is "chasing after someone else's rainbow." Codependents completely neglect themselves and the satisfaction of their own wants, needs, and desires. As they see themselves, they have only one value and purpose: to service another person's wants and needs. That other person becomes the sole raison d'être of a codependent's life. And as this self-negation gathers momentum, a codependent's identity becomes buried in the other person.

" 'What time is it?' may sound like a simple question to you, but to a codependent like me, it requires a series of mental gymnastics," explains Frannie. "I have to quickly ask myself, 'What time does *he want* it to be?' If I think he wants it to be early, I say, 'It's only six o'clock.' But if I think he wants it to be later, I answer, 'It's already six o'clock.' It never occurs to me to just state the time, 'Six o'clock.' I always feel I have to give *him* the answer *he* wants to hear."

The tendency of individual codependents to undervalue themselves usually becomes established long before adulthood. Like the majority of alcoholics, most codependents grew up in addictive households. Alcoholic and codependent parents in-

still in their children values of responsibility, loyalty, selflessness, taking care of others, and helpfulness. But in the chaos of
addictive families, these selfless virtues become overvalued.
During their formative years, codependents learn to take these
positive, helping traits to self-destructive extremes: responsible
becomes hyperresponsible, loyalty becomes blind devotion,
and selflessness becomes self-negation. Because they have been
taught to put other people's needs before their own, codependents become martyrs and victims in their own lives.

If you grew up codependent, you no doubt have carried
these teachings into your adult relationships. Codependent attitudes may have not only ruled your relationship with the
alcoholic, but have spilled over into other relationships as well.
You may constantly feel as if you need to do everything for
everybody in your life. You may give other people too much
power to influence the way you behave, think, and feel.

"I'm very aware of how my extreme dependency on Leonard
gets played out in our relationship," confides Celia, talking
about her boyfriend, who has been sober in AA for two years.
"And I can clearly see how much this codependency is similar
to the relationship I had with my alcoholic father. But now,
I'm starting to realize that my codependency exists in other
areas of my life. I am very codependent on the job, and I
always have been. I become totally preoccupied with my boss's
moods. If she's having a bad day, I have a bad day. If she's
having a good day, I have a good day. My mood depends
entirely on hers."

As an Eye-Opener, you need to pay attention to the way
codependency has affected all your relationships. Gaining
awareness is one of the major tasks of the Eye-Opener stage of
relationship recovery. Now that you've recognized the impact
of the alcoholic's disease on your current relationship, you're
ready to examine codependent relationships from your past. In
retracing the past, see if you can uncover any roots that under-
lie your current codependent relationship or relationships. Although insight about the origins of your codependency may
not change anything right away, it can help you begin to lay

the groundwork for healthier and happier relationships tomorrow.

Just as neither you nor the alcoholic in your life can develop a lifetime "cure" for addiction, you cannot reverse your codependency through any "quick-fix" methods. Indeed, you may always have the urge to fall back into familiar codependent patterns in your relationships. But now that you are aware of these patterns, you can recognize self-destructive behavior for what it is. Whenever you see these codependent patterns of thought, feeling, or behavior, you will know to do what you can to stop them—and to seek help from others in your efforts.

The most effective treatment for codependency involves treating yourself to an examined life. True, without change, awareness of codependency is only half the battle. But awareness will help you focus on the aspects of yourself and your relationships that most need improvement. Guided by this new consciousness, you can transform yourself into a more independent person and your relationships into more satisfying partnerships between equals. Codependency will always get in the way of mutually fulfilling relationships. But as you become less codependent, you will take the first big steps toward transforming your relationships.

SETTING NEW RULES

Whether you grew up in an alcoholic home, moved into one as an adult, or both, you have learned a number of lessons that you will have to unlearn in recovery. In her ground-breaking book *It Will Never Happen to Me!*, Claudia Black names three rules that every family member observes when one or more of them has an addiction: "Don't talk, don't trust, and don't feel." If you have grown up or lived with an alcoholic, these rules probably became second nature to you. Closed-down or cutoff communication, constant suspicions or misgivings, and repressed or "stuffed" emotions may have seemed like the only ways for you—and your family or relationship—to survive. In the atmosphere of unending crises created by addiction, most people turn to silence and repression in a futile attempt to keep things under control.

The rules that forbid talking, trusting, and feeling become law in alcoholic households because codependents who are caught up in the web of alcoholism try hard to normalize the instability created by the disease. Trying to make sure problems don't get out of hand, codependents work overtime to rescue and protect the alcoholic or other family members. They may call up a boss with an excuse for the alcoholic's absence or clean up the alcoholic's vomit and put him or her to bed. Most codependents will do everything they can to ease the pain, stop the crisis, and protect those who seem threatened by the disease. In trying to do the "right" thing by keeping the problem under control, though, family members tend to push the problem underground. However much they want to improve the alcoholic's situation, their efforts always backfire. And though well intentioned, their actions unfortunately "enable" the alcoholism to remain hidden. In most cases, the alcoholic becomes more and more irresponsible as codependents accept more and more responsibilities.

Alcoholic families and relationships operate under the delusion that the best way to handle crises is to pretend these disasters do not exist. For the mirage of "normalcy" to remain intact, everyone has to play by the rules of no talking, no trusting, and no feeling. For this reason, anyone who tries to break the rules of an alcoholic family quickly meets the wrath of other family members. Everyone reinforces the rules because any breakdown of the facade would mean admitting that a problem exists. And no one in an alcoholic relationship wants to admit this "awful truth."

In recovery, when alcoholics and those who love them finally stop their denial, they need to establish new rules for their relationships. The rules that seemed to make sense when the alcoholic was drinking make no sense in sobriety. Once you have recognized the disease of alcoholism, you will need to scrap all the rules that formerly contributed to your denial of the problem. Other enabling rules, which were invented to help protect the active alcoholic but inadvertently supported the chemical dependency instead, must also go. To replace these obsolete rules of denial and enabling, you will need to develop new rules of awareness and mutual self-sufficiency.

"One of the hardest things I ever did was to stay out of my husband's and children's recovery," confesses Jean, who told me that her main rule before recovery was to take care of everything and everyone in her family. "I wanted to know which program—Al-Anon or NACOA [National Association of Children of Alcoholics]—would be best for the girls. And I wanted to know the best AA meetings for my husband to go to. I was afraid that if he didn't get to the 'right' meetings, he might drop out of the program altogether and start drinking again.

"I'm beginning to see that I can't take care of anyone's recovery except my own. My daughters are almost grown up now. They can try both programs and make their own decisions. And Sam can go to lots of meetings until he finds the ones he likes best. Meanwhile, I have to focus on *my* recovery program."

The new rules of awareness and mutual self-sufficiency support the most important overall rule of recovery: to take responsibility for yourself—and yourself alone. Trying to take charge of other people's lives not only gives you an extra burden you certainly don't need, but it relieves others of any responsibility for their actions. Only by giving up this rule of hyperresponsibility and overprotectiveness can you—and the alcoholic—hope to change in any enduring and meaningful way.

The process of breaking old rules and establishing new ones requires time, patience, and tolerance. For one thing, you may not *really* be sure you want to change the rules of your relationship. Your sense of identity and feelings of importance and self-worth may be tangled up in obsolete rules like hyperresponsibility. To stay on a course of positive change, you will need to keep reminding yourself that these old codependent rules stand in the way of your getting better. So for now, just concentrate on stopping—on breaking away from your old rules—and just observe the primary rule of accountability: *Each person is solely responsible for his or her own recovery.* With time and effort, you'll figure out, through trial and error, what other rules work or don't work in your new relationships.

CONFRONTING SELF-DESTRUCTIVE BEHAVIOR

When one person in a family makes a remarkable recovery from alcoholism or addiction, it is unfortunately not unusual for someone else in the family to start getting sicker. The long buildup of unexpressed rage and resentment can sometimes propel people into self-destructive activity. So, while the alcoholic is getting better, another family member may "suddenly" exhibit signs of addiction, alcoholism, compulsiveness, or some other self-destructive behavior. Some of this "new" self-destructive behavior may have existed all the time. But perhaps no one noticed it next to the more blatant addiction in the family.

"I was a teenager when my father first got sober," recalls Sandy, an attractive newspaper reporter. "I remember feeling very resentful about it. Sure, *now* he was interested in my comings and goings. Before he had never asked about anything, and now he wanted to be a responsible father. My mother had always asked and known my whereabouts; she deserved that right. But I felt he had a real nerve asking these questions after being totally oblivious about my life for so many years of drinking. I had always been somewhat obsessed with food, but I started binging and purging regularly when he sobered up. I guess I was taking my resentments out on myself."

The seeds of Sandy's eating disorder—her insecurity, unvoiced anger and resentment, the obsession with food—had been hidden since puberty. But when her father sobered up, the problem got much worse—as if she allowed herself to get sicker now that the rest of the family finally had the time to notice. Often, given the new recovery environment that frees up the family's attention, another family member may unconsciously try to claim some time under the spotlight that once fell only on the alcoholic.

The self-destructive behavior of other family members in the Eye-Opener stage of the alcoholic's recovery may also aim to retain the familiar chaos of the addictive environment. Family members can become so accustomed to relating to one another according to the rigid system of rules demanded in a chaotic atmosphere that they only feel comfortable interacting in that way. To recapture this "comfortable discomfort," some family members may unconsciously adopt self-destructive behavior that re-creates the customary pandemonium in their lives.

"My mother stopped drinking when I was eighteen, and I immediately quit school and took off for Europe with very little money and no idea of what I wanted to do there," remembers Joan, who at twenty-eight regularly attends meetings of Adult Children of Alcoholics to help keep her recovery on track. "I think what I really wanted to do was to find some wild and crazy times just like the ones I knew so well. Getting sober had shaken up the family balance. So as my parents got better, I got worse. I started courting my own instability. Today, I know that sort of thing is pretty typical in alcoholic families. But at the time, it didn't make any sense at all."

Like Joan's chaotic adventure in Europe, a codependent's self-destructive behavior may merely be a temporary reaction to the new circumstances of sobriety. But sometimes, as Sandy's eating disorder did, this behavior can also signal a more serious deep-seated problem. When no one in the family has the time or energy to pay attention to these "secondary" problems, those who suffer from them usually try, as best they can, to keep the problems in check. But when the alcoholic begins to pursue sobriety, the addictions and compulsions of other family members often surface. These problems demand immediate action as soon as you become aware of them. Fortunately, now that you have been alerted to the presence of alcoholism, you have a newly awakened consciousness of addictions and compulsions. If you recognize the possible onset of your own or another codependent's addiction—to food, shopping, smoking, drugs, alcohol, or anything else—seek help quickly. A "new" addiction not only threatens to drag your family or your relationship back into the dark world of sickness and denial, but it may threaten your life. To recover from this new addiction, as well as the old, you will need to seek help immediately from a professional, a self-help group, or both. The Resource Organizations section of this book lists a number of organizations that can help you overcome these addictions or compulsions.

Checking for Obsessions and Compulsions

You may wonder whether some of your thoughts are obsessive or some of your behavior is compulsive. Consider any thoughts that regularly preoccupy you or activities that seem to demand a great deal of your time or effort. First, make a list of all the repetitive things you do or thoughts that take hold of your mind. Don't bother listing general activities like work or sleep or everyday thoughts like vague financial concerns. Concentrate on more specific thoughts or behavior that you seem to think or do the same way every time. For example, do you wash your hands many times during the course of a day? Do you check the front door a few times to make sure you locked it? Do you have several drinks whenever you have a business lunch? Do you constantly worry about whether the alcoholic will pick up another drink? Do you have sexual fantasies about every new person you meet? These are examples of compulsive behavior and obsessive thinking.

Write down the amount of time, daily and weekly, that you spend on each of these thoughts or activities. Has any thought or activity taken up more than an hour's time each day, and has it persisted for longer than three weeks? If so, you need to get some feedback from a professional counselor who specializes in addictive behaviors or from someone else you trust deeply, perhaps a sponsor from your self-help group. Almost everyone experiences periods when certain thoughts weigh heavily on the mind or certain behaviors become part of a routine. But if these preoccupations take up a great deal of time over an extended period of weeks or months, they have gotten out of control. Share your list of preoccupations with someone you trust. That person can tell you whether you have legitimate cause for concern.

If you need treatment for an obsession, compulsion, or addiction, help is available. Many clinics and hotlines specialize in particular disorders, so check your telephone yellow pages, self-help directories, and the list of resource organizations in this book. Most of these specialized programs have developed questionnaires, so you can double-check to make sure your problem warrants professional attention. In any case, if you need help, get it. As an Eye-Opener, you need to make a commitment to end denial and to stop compulsive behavior of any kind. And since you can only change yourself, this means your own behavior, not the alcoholic's. If you need any further motivation, just remind yourself that no real relationships can exist in the presence of addiction. So unless you've started recovering from yours, it's a waste of time to turn your attention to your relationships.

RECOGNIZING BURIED FEELINGS

For years, both you and the addict have probably been observing the "Don't Feel" rule. Since they made you feel uncomfortable, you most likely buried any hostile feelings toward each other, hoping that they would go away. But anger, resentment, distrust, and depression will not disappear just because you wish them away. Sooner or later, these feelings have to surface. If you cannot vent these emotions, you will never put this part of the past behind you. And you can't continue to carry around all that old baggage if you want to make a fresh start in your relationship.

"People kept telling me that sooner or later I would feel angry toward Barbara, but all I really felt were sadness and pity," explains Troy, an accountant whose wife joined AA eight months ago. "Then, just the other day, I suddenly found myself really furious at her. All this stuff I had completely forgotten just came pouring out. I started to think about how her alcoholism had disrupted my life. I felt like I had been putting my life on hold for ten years because of her disease, and I was fuming."

Addiction leaves lasting scars, but sometimes the wounds run so deep that you may not even see them at first. If you keep your eyes open, however, they will soon be apparent. You could not help but get wounded as you tried to fight an un-winnable battle against another person's addiction. You could never force the addict into sobriety, and you couldn't get better yourself—not as long as you were fighting someone else's bat-tle instead of your own. In the Eye-Opener stage of your recov-ery, you may just be beginning to realize, as Troy did, how much time you wasted in trying to "save" the alcoholic. So don't be surprised if you experience an explosion of anger, intense depression, or both.

To defeat your depression and move through your anger, you will need to recognize and accept that they both are part of the recovery process. It's perfectly normal to feel red hot or blue in the Eye-Opener stage of recovery. As you move through this stage, you will become more and more aware of these feelings. And although you will certainly find this new awareness painful, these feelings will linger forever unless you confront them. You have to recognize and acknowledge these emotions if you want them to go away.

When codependents in the Eye-Opener stage of recovery first allow their emotions to surface, these feelings may rush out in an uncontrollable flood. You may, for example, be plagued by fits of uncontrollable sobbing that make it impossible for you to do anything else. Or you may feel so enraged that you want to act out this anger through attacks on the alcoholic, yourself, or others. Although you can certainly expect long-buried emotions to be volatile when they surface, you will probably benefit from professional help if they become uncontrollable. Psychotherapy can give you the opportunity to release these pent-up emotions in a safe place and in a nondestructive manner. To help you get through this difficult period, try to realize that these feelings won't last forever. Recovery will help you heal these wounds.

Unburied Feelings

How many of the following feelings have you experienced in the past week?

agitation	emptiness	loneliness
anger	envy	low self-esteem
anguish	exasperation	mood swings
annoyance	fear	numbness
anxiety	frustration	panic
bitterness	futility	rage
confusion	guardedness	regret
contempt	guilt	resentment
defeat	helplessness	sadness
dejection	hopelessness	self-doubt
depression	hostility	self-loathing
despair	humiliation	self-reproach
disappointment	hurt	shame
disapproval	inferiority	sorrow
disdain	irritability	uncertainty
disgust	isolation	victimization
embarrassment	jealousy	worthlessness
	lethargy	

Check off the feelings on the list that you identify with today. Then, every few weeks, take out the list and see if any of these feelings have disappeared. Cross out any of those that you no longer feel.

Again, it's not "bad" to have any of these feelings. You may have good reason to feel angry, or victimized, or uncertain, or sad. Indeed, each of these feelings is typical among Eye-Openers. But if you allow these feelings to linger and fester under your surface calm, they will burden you and retard your recovery. You need to recognize these feelings, admit them for the first time, and start dealing with them instead of burying them.

To help move through your anger and depression, you may want to balance the feelings in the list by making a list of the positive or uplifting feelings that you are experiencing in recovery for the first time, or at least for the first time in a long time. Watch for the reemergence of long-forgotten feelings, such as joy, gratitude, contentment, playfulness, self-confidence, happiness, eagerness, wholeness, and love. If you get stuck, you will find more positive feelings listed in Chapter 4. In charting the progression of your emotions in recovery, you will see that as "negative" feelings decrease, "positive" ones increase. You will find it inspiring to keep a record of how much better you feel as you continue to work your recovery program. You will have the proof right before you: Eye-Openers don't have to stay depressed and angry; they can move from darkness to light.

Another exercise that may help you accentuate the positive is to develop a "day's-end diary." In the diary you can list the things that you did or things that happened to you today that you feel good about. For example, you may have changed the oil in your car for the first time or helped your daughter puzzle out a tough algebra problem. Perhaps your partner gave you a present just for being yourself. The "day's-end diary" can help as you move through your anger and depression. By acknowledging the things in your daily life of which you are proud or for which you are grateful, you will remind yourself that even though you may feel enraged or saddened now, good things do exist that can help ease these bad feelings. Eye-Openers need to work on increasing their awareness not only of the negative reality of illness in their lives, but of the positive reality of recovery. By counting the things for which you are grateful, you will gather the strength you need to stay on the road to individual and relationship recovery.

MOURNING OVER LOSSES

Believe it or not, you may actually feel badly about the loss of your codependency. You may want to recapture the old chaotic way of life, even after you have chosen to leave it behind. Why should you feel so unhappy now that, as an Eye-Opener, you're finally moving toward the kind of life and relationships you've always hoped for? Because in declaring an end to codependency, you are pulling a shroud over the only life you've ever known. Especially if you grew up in an addictive household, codependency may have played a part in all your relationships, as a child *and* as an adult. It's not easy to leave behind something you've known throughout your life, no matter how self-destructive it may be.

Despite the many positive changes in your early recovery from codependency, the alcoholic's new sobriety, and the beginning of your new relationship, you may experience the end of illness as a terrible loss. Even the worst relationships and worst situations have some redeeming features—aspects you may miss in recovery. Although you need to put the old relationship, with all its insanity, behind you, you may have become somewhat attached to that old craziness. You may or may not attempt to reproduce this craziness as Joan did, through your own chaotic adventures. But you will almost certainly miss the excitement. As Philip, a lawyer who came to me for counseling, admits, "Life was never boring when my wife was drinking. But now she's sober, it is kind of boring." Life before recovery may have been wired, but wires almost always deliver a charge. The addict's life, your life, and the life you share together may seem a little dull by comparison.

"When Steven was still drinking and doing cocaine, life was a roller coaster. I never knew what to expect," says Kathy, a stockbroker whose husband has been sober for two months. "He was a wild and crazy addict. On a moment's notice, he might charter a boat and take a dozen people to Block Island for dinner or hire a big band for a friend's small birthday party. Once when he took me shopping for a new coat, I thought we were just going downtown to Saks, but he took me to Paris. And surprises like that weren't at all unusual for him.

"Things certainly seem dull now in comparison. I was always worried sick about his next big fiasco, and I don't miss that at all. But now the most exciting thing he wants to do is go to an afternoon movie. Evenings, of course, are saved for his meetings. In the past, I was always waiting for the other shoe to drop. Now I'm just waiting, for what I really don't know. I feel like something is missing. Maybe it's just the high drama."

People in addictive relationships often grow accustomed to the high drama supplied by the addiction. During the active period of the disease, the alcoholic, the star of the show, always stood at center stage. The alcoholic took all the action, while the supporting cast around him had nothing to do except provide well-rehearsed reactions. No wonder the stage seems dark and the drama ended once the active alcoholic exits. The show may have been awful, but it never failed to hold your attention. After all the theatrics, recovery may seem anticlimactic.

Like Kathy, you may miss the drama and excitement of life with an active alcoholic or addict. Or you may have become attached to some other feature of your codependency and the alcoholic's addiction. You may, for instance, miss the familiar roles that played a part in your life together for so many years. Or now that the addict has turned to others for help, you may miss the comfortable illusion that only you could save the alcoholic. No matter what aspect of your old life together *you* miss, you will experience it as a grievous loss.

Since you are leaving behind so much of your past life in illness, loss is a necessary part of the recovery process. The loss of your familiar role in an all-too-familiar scenario will create a void in your life. When you, as an Eye-Opener, first recognize this emptiness, mourning will be necessary and appropriate. Although mourning takes time, you can take action to help move through your grief. Most people find it helpful to try the following:

- Share the pain of grieving. Talk to friends, people in recovery meetings, and professional counselors. Those who have suffered the same wounds and those who have helped others work through similar periods of mourning will be understanding of your grief.
- Don't allow yourself to be lonely. Call friends. Arrange to do something fun with someone else.
- Say what you need when you need it. Most people are happy to help a friend in need. But they first need to know that you're in a rough spot and need help to get out.
- Develop other interests outside your relationship with the recovering alcoholic. Getting involved in new activities and meeting new people can fill some of the empty spaces in your life.
- Give of yourself. Do something nice for someone who is less fortunate than you. You may be surprised what you receive in return. When you give from the heart, you will feel more generous, useful, and productive and less self-centered.
- Treat yourself! Do something extra special for yourself at least once a day. Indulge yourself: buy flowers, take a warm bath, get a massage, give yourself an extra hour of sleep, take a cab to work.

The grief Kathy described earlier was a fairly typical reaction to the losses brought about by her husband's recovery. While his addiction was in full swing, his drinking and snorting served as the departure point for all the excitement in their lives. And addiction took up so much time and energy from their lives that they never got around to making many friends or finding other interests or diversions. Now that they're in recovery, they need to move through their grief by forming new friendships that can provide an outlet for their pain and help them continue to move forward in healthy ways. But they will also have to find new sources of excitement in their lives —individually and as a couple. They both need to learn new ways to have fun—by treating themselves or enjoying new thrills—while remaining sober.

Fortunately, in most cases it only takes time for this sort of healing to occur. Dealing with your emerging anger and depression, discussed earlier in this chapter, will play an important part in this grieving process. Finally confronting these hidden feelings will allow you to put them where they belong: in the past. If you work on your anger and depression and try some of the methods of relieving grief suggested earlier, you will speed the grieving process.

It is critical to move through your grief if you truly want to put the past behind you. The fact that you miss certain aspects of alcoholism or codependency is one of the major forces that can pull you back into the disease. To guard against backsliding, you need to draw a clear line between your life and relationships in disease and those in recovery. The following exercise, in helping you tackle the causes of your grief directly, may clarify this line between past and present: Divide a piece of paper into two columns. Write "Losses of Codependency" at the top of the first column and "Alternatives" at the top of the second column. In the first column, list anything you miss about your codependency. Include any benefit you think you might have gotten from the illness. (Kathy, for instance, put "excitement" at the top of her list of losses.) You may list "being needed," or "a feeling of importance," or anything else that codependency or alcoholism gave you. In the second column, write one or more activities that may help restore some of what you've lost. (Kathy wrote "travel," "skiing," and "throwing a surprise party for Steven's ninetieth day of sobriety.") As much as you can, try to make the activities in the second column a regular part of your new life in recovery.

Incorporating new activities in your life will help reinforce the notion that except for some temporary lapses, the codependent part of your life has ended. Once you strongly believe it, you will have completed the grief process. When you can officially pronounce the old relationship between you dead and buried, you can begin to turn your attention to building a new relationship.

2

KEEPING THE PAST BEHIND YOU

Practicing Recovery

If you are an Eye-Opener, you are in luck. Fortunately for you, no matter how confusing or frightening the path to recovery may seem, you do not have to travel this road alone. Many have gone before you, and many will join you on the same journey now. You no longer have to do everything alone. All you really need to do is be willing to reach out your hand to others—good friends, people in your support group, professionals, and perhaps even the alcoholic—and say, "I'm in recovery." Most of these people will gladly accept your hand. From them, you can draw support during the rough times ahead, and with them, you can also share all the good times to come.

CHOOSING YOUR RECOVERY PROGRAM

A recovery program—whether it's a self-help group like Al-Anon or AA, individual therapy, group therapy, or any combination of these programs—can put you in touch with many of your supporters. Support groups and other "recovery aides" can help guide and encourage your pursuit of recovery. As you alter the nature of your life, members of self-help groups, therapists, and good friends will all do their best to break your fall when you slip and then help put you back on your feet again.

A recovery program will help you advance your personal and relationship recovery in many ways. It can provide the safe environment you need to feel your feelings, share your secret thoughts, and learn to trust—all, perhaps, for the first time.

"John and I have been married for twenty-five years," confides Gladys, a librarian, "but it's only now that we're both in recovery programs that I feel we are making serious changes. I feel like I'm getting stronger every day and he's getting more sensitive. For the first time in many, many years, we're really starting to be emotionally available to each other. You wouldn't believe the difference it makes."

Old wounds do heal, but they need a period of healing and good medication. By far the best medicine for alcoholics is AA, and the best medicine for those who love them is Al-Anon. Self-help groups will give you the opportunity to talk with people who know and appreciate exactly what you are saying because they are experiencing—or have experienced in the past—similar circumstances, feelings, and thoughts. These parallels allow members of self-help groups to listen and understand in a way that a still-active alcoholic—or even a newly recovering alcoholic—cannot. At self-help meetings you can begin to voice your feelings. With time and practice, you will grow more comfortable with yourself and your feelings. This new sense of confidence and ease will allow you to carry your ability to share out of the meetings. You will approach your relationships with the recovering alcoholic and other important people in your life with a new honesty and openness.

Self-help groups may not be for everyone, but they have already helped a great many people. In the United States today, membership in self-help groups has soared to an estimated fifteen million people! If you have doubts about whether Al-Anon is right for you, I strongly encourage you to go to at least five meetings before deciding whether you like the program. (Indeed, most programs that are modeled after AA recommend that you attend even more meetings—ninety in ninety days—before you make any judgment about whether a particular group will help you.) If your community is large enough to have several different groups, try them all to see whether you like the dynamics of one group better than the others. Even if you gave a self-help group a fair shake once before and hated it, try attending again every few weeks. Meetings and those who attend them change regularly, but what is even more important, so do you. Because your changes may provide you with a new perspective, give a particular recovery program more than one chance. What you hated yesterday, you may love today.

Many recovering codependents and alcoholics can also benefit from professional therapy. I recommend individual or group therapy or both to most codependents and alcoholics in the Eye-Opener stage of recovery (and often in later stages as well). Psychotherapists who understand the diseases of alcoholism and codependency can offer you professional guidance as you try to understand and dramatically alter the patterns of your life. If you temporarily need an authority figure to make you feel more confident about the new direction in your life, you may draw comfort from the psychological expertise that informs a professional's advice and suggestions for change. In addition to offering you an understanding ear, a psychotherapist may make you feel more certain about her or his confidentiality. Although, as you will surely discover, self-help programs will also offer you complete confidentiality, you may not yet have enough trust to feel comfortable about sharing your "personal secrets" with a large group. That's okay. Give yourself time to develop the ability to trust more and more people.

If you decide that you need professional therapy to work out some of the difficulties of recovery, however, it is critical that the psychotherapist you choose have knowledge and experience in dealing with alcoholism and the family. A qualified therapist can help you evaluate whether individual or group therapy or both are appropriate for you at a particular time. In most cases, I advise my clients to put off couples counseling until they have first addressed the primary difficulties of alcoholism and codependency.

Group therapy may offer you a safe place to begin to share your feelings with others. Although some people quickly feel comfortable speaking in large self-help groups, others need to practice in smaller groups first. Therapy groups, generally limited to fewer than ten members, can provide Eye-Openers with an opportunity to rehearse their openness with a small number of people. In addition, the same people attend every group session, a circumstance that tends to foster the development of trust among the members. Finally, therapy groups offer the guidance of professional therapists, who often provide useful suggestions based on their expertise in addictions and codependency.

Although I recommend both individual and group therapy to most Eye-Openers, I also strongly urge them to work on their Al-Anon or AA recovery programs at the same time. Self-help groups and professional therapy complement each other well. Unlike most therapy groups, for instance, Al-Anon meetings consist *entirely* of people who are recovering from codependency. Even before you feel comfortable speaking in a self-help group, listening to others talk about their experiences will show you that you are not alone. You will learn that other people have had feelings and have survived crises similar to your own. By listening to the experiences of others, you will gain hope, knowing that things can and will get better if you take the initiative to change.

As an Eye-Opener—and later as a Pioneer in recovery—you and the alcoholic in your life will need to work on building a firm foundation of recovery within yourselves. This foundation will securely support your later efforts to confront the complicated "relationship problems" in the Mutual-Partner stage. Even though you both almost certainly have problems relating to each other as a couple, you will probably find it most effective to postpone couples or family counseling until you have built this new foundation for your relationships. Of course, there are times when couples therapy may be essential in earlier phases of recovery. Sometimes crises cannot be delayed. You may face critical decisions about the future of your relationship or about parenting. You may be in danger of splitting up permanently. Or you may find yourself in an abusive situation. These types of crises demand immediate professional input. Again, a therapist who is experienced in treating addictions and the family can advise you about what kind of therapy you need most—and when to get it.

Therapy, like recovery, should be flexible. Try to keep your options open in choosing helpers for your recovery. By drawing on all the many resources available to you in the early phase of recovery, you can begin to change the direction of your life.

THE TWELVE STEPS: LIGHTING A PATH TO RECOVERY

Although I strongly recommend Al-Anon and AA to any family or couple who is recovering from the influence of alcoholism, you may choose not to become part of a formal program modeled after the Twelve Steps of AA and Al-Anon. Even if you decide not to take advantage of the benefits that come with participating in a self-help group, however, you would be wise to look to the Twelve Steps as a philosophical guide. The Twelve Steps can be valuable tools of recovery even when divorced from the many self-help groups that focus on its principles. However, the "we" of the fellowship cannot be underestimated.

THE TWELVE STEPS OF ALCOHOLICS ANONYMOUS

1. We admitted we were powerless over alcohol—that our lives had become unmanageable.

2. Came to believe that a Power greater than ourselves could restore us to sanity.
3. Made a decision to turn our will and our lives over to the care of God, *as we understood Him.*
4. Made a searching and fearless moral inventory of ourselves.
5. Admitted to God, to ourselves, and to another human being the exact nature of our wrongs.
6. Were entirely ready to have God remove all these defects of character.
7. Humbly asked Him to remove our shortcomings.
8. Made a list of all persons we had harmed, and became willing to make amends to them all.
9. Made direct amends to such people whenever possible, except when to do so would injure them or others.
10. Continued to take personal inventory and when we were wrong promptly admitted it.
11. Sought through prayer and meditation to improve our conscious contact with God *as we understood Him,* praying only for knowledge of His will for us and the power to carry that out.
12. Having had a spiritual awakening as the result of these steps, we tried to carry this message to alcoholics* and to practice these principles in all our affairs.

The Twelve Steps provide a blueprint for living, a tool that can help us sort out the things we can and cannot control in our lives. The Twelve Steps will help you take responsibility for the actions that are truly in your control. At the same time, they will help you leave behind your need for perfectionism (perfect control over yourself) and for control over other people. The Twelve Steps provide only a suggested guide—*not* an indisputable rule book—for living life one day at a time. But if you work on them, really work on making them an essential part of your life, they will work for you. Try to use them as governing principles on a day-to-day basis. If you do, the Twelve Steps can become a yardstick of your personal growth and spiritual development in recovery, measuring your con-

---

* Al-Anon substitutes "others" for "alcoholics" in the Twelfth Step.

tinuing progress—instead of your "failure" to achieve the impossible dream of perfection.

Perhaps you think you have already "done" the Twelve Steps at some point in your life. But the steps are never done completely, once and for all. The steps toward recovery often require retracing and reapplication. One day, you may focus on "envy" and "jealousy" as your character defects in working on Steps Four through Ten; on a different day, you may identify "anger" and "resentment" as your major flaws. Or you may make a special effort to apply the steps to one particular arena of your life at a time: at work, for example, or in your interaction with sales clerks, service people, and others you know only as acquaintances. The more recovery you achieve, the more aware you will become of other shortcomings or problems you want to improve.

Before you sought recovery, you were probably static— stuck in the same place over and over again. But now that you have started to get better, neither you nor your recovery is static. You are dynamic, constantly changing for the better, it is hoped, most of the time. For this reason, the Twelve Steps were designed as flexible guidelines. As you become healthier through your own recovery, you can adapt the Twelve Steps to your changing needs. In this way you will continue to improve. And when you see the miracle of your own change happening right before your eyes, you may begin to have faith in a power higher than yourself.

POWERLESSNESS: GIVING UP CONTROL

One of the secrets to stopping old, outmoded behaviors like alcoholism and codependency involves admitting your essential powerlessness in many areas of your life. As an Eye-Opener, you need to take the time to recognize your powerlessness to control all but your own actions. As you will discover, by admitting your powerlessness, you can actually gain power. This apparent paradox is easily resolved, for in actuality, all you are giving up is false power.

Codependents (and alcoholics, too) operate under an illusion of control. Active alcoholics and codependents involve themselves in a muddle of manipulation and maneuvering in a vain attempt to control the people, places, and things around them. They think that by trying to fix everything and everybody (or by escaping into a bottle), they can gain a measure of control over their lives. They hope that by trying to make other people or things better, they will feel better themselves. But actually, they end up doing nothing more than chasing rainbows.

By closing your eyes to this mirage, you can open your eyes to the real power you have to change your life. Recognizing that you cannot control things outside yourself, you gain a renewed sense of control over your life. If you admit the existence of a higher power than yourself, you will no longer feel obliged to try to control things you cannot really control anyway. You will no longer have to try to fix things that either don't need fixing or don't need *you* to fix them. As a wise person once said, "You can find real power in your powerlessness."

Letting go of your need to control and learning to live life on life's terms is one of the biggest lessons of recovery. Most recovering codependents and alcoholics find this lesson particularly difficult because it demands so much trust and an enormous leap of faith. To accept your own powerlessness, you need to accept that if there is indeed some "master plan" for the future, it rests in a power higher than you. You will need to put your trust in a Higher Power—God, Fate, Al-Anon, the love of your friends and family, the overall process of recovery, or some other power greater than you alone—that will make sure that everything comes out all right.

"I wish I could just remember how much better things are when I move to the back of the bus rather than try to drive it," admits Jim, whose obsession with control has prevented him from asking others for the help he needs. "It feels like no matter how hard I try to let go of my control, I'm always trying to take it back again.

"I know that this thing I have about control started a long time ago. I grew up in the city and I got pretty street smart. I prided myself on being very independent. I thought I could handle anything. So it's still hard for me not to be in charge.

"I've been going to Al-Anon meetings for ten months now, but I still haven't gotten a phone number or asked anyone to sponsor me. It just feels like I'll be totally out of control of my whole life if I have to ask for help. But I'm just getting more and more miserable the way I am. As long as I'm trying to control the world, I know I'll never be at peace with myself."

Eye-Openers need to allow themselves to get out of the driver's seat for once and simply enjoy the ride. If you're like Jim, you need to realize that you'll never have a chance to recover fully until you admit that you can't handle everything alone. In refusing to recognize your essential powerlessness to recover completely on your own, you are simultaneously refusing to accept help from a Higher Power and from other people. It's a vicious circle: As long as you continue to try to get better entirely on your own, you will never allow yourself to ask for help. And unless you reach out for help from a Higher Power and others, you will remain isolated and alone.

Are you still trying to control almost everything—and everyone—in your life? When the disease of alcoholism rules a household, the alcoholic tries to control the drinking while codependents try to control not only the alcoholic's drinking, but everything else as well. This powerful need to control most often masks a strong fear of being or appearing out of control. Although these attempts at control sometimes work as a stopgap, they ultimately succeed only in disguising the real problem of alcoholism. And as the disease progresses, everyone in the household loses more and more control.

The compulsion to control doesn't work any better in recovery. With your new understanding of the disease, you will need to accept that you cannot control the alcoholic's recovery, just as you cannot control anyone else's actions. The recovery process—for both codependents and alcoholics—is based on the principles of powerlessness and the surrender of willfulness.

"I have to keep telling myself that I'm powerless over people, places, and things," admits Nancy, a twenty-nine-year-old nurse who hasn't found this challenge particularly easy to master. "In my relationship with my husband, I'm always wishing he would be exactly the way I want him to be. I have to try to accept Kenny for who he is and where he is in his recovery.

"I guess I just have to let things happen as they will instead of trying to manipulate everything to come out the way I want it to. Whenever I try to force things to happen, they don't happen that way. Actually, the harder I try to impose my will, the worse things usually turn out. I'm slowly learning to stop trying to make things happen and just let them happen. When I can relax and really let things go, they usually turn out just fine."

Like Nancy, you may have difficulty accepting your power-lessness and letting things go. So whenever you feel compelled to try to control the alcoholic's recovery, every aspect of your child's experience inside and outside the home, or anything else outside yourself, stop and ask yourself the following question: "What is the worst possible thing that can happen if I don't control x, y, and z?" In many cases, the answer may surprise you. The "worst thing" may not be such a bad thing after all. You'll realize that the world won't fall apart just because you give up control over it. By beginning to put things in perspective in this way, Eye-Openers can start to sort out the things that they should try to influence from the things that are truly out of their control.

Many people in recovery find the Serenity Prayer helpful in directing their efforts to let go of things that are out of their control. The Serenity Prayer states: "God grant me the serenity to accept the things I cannot change, the courage to change the things I can, and the wisdom to know the difference." If you find this a wise philosophy, memorize the prayer. It will come in handy in those moments when you desperately want to control someone or something that's not in your control. By repeating it softly or silently to yourself, you will begin the process of sorting out the things you can control from the things you are powerless to change.

Using the Serenity Prayer to help acknowledge your powerlessness will relieve a lot of the anxiety you may feel. Most anxiety arises from a fear of the future, which members of support groups call "projection." But living in the future is not really living at all; it's just waiting, paralyzed by a sense of foreboding. Repeating the Serenity Prayer can help you realize that you have no control over the future. Certainly you can think about the future, make plans, and take steps to further your goals. But you are essentially powerless to determine everything that will happen tomorrow. You can't *make* things happen exactly the way you want them to happen, so you may as well let be the things that are beyond your control. You will never live up to your potential today if you have your head in tomorrow's clouds. So let the future take care of itself. Just try to take care of yourself, doing the best you can, *today*. When you admit your powerlessness over the future, you will stop projecting so much. You will free yourself, to live today to the fullest.

"I accept the fact now that I have no control over my wife's alcoholism," Andrew, an antiques dealer, explains with relief. "But I sometimes deny the fact that I can't control other things and other people in my life. I know that what I have to work on now is learning acceptance in *all* areas of my life.

"My sponsor in Al-Anon keeps telling me to accept life on life's terms. I need to stop trying to change those things that bother me, but are really none of my business. My business is me and my own attitudes and actions, nobody else's. Whenever I want things, people, or situations to be different from what they are, I get really angry. But that's just a lot of wasted emotion. My recovery is greatest when I can say that whatever happens today is just how it's supposed to be. Then I feel good."

Recognizing your powerlessness also demands that you trust others as well as a higher power. You will need to trust that the people in your life are capable of living their lives without your constant direction. You can offer suggestions, but ultimately you have to allow others to find their own solutions. You will have to trust the alcoholic, for instance, to take care of her or his own recovery. Because you are powerless to control another person's recovery, you will need to trust that a higher power, the alcoholic's sponsor in the recovery program, and friends will supply the direction needed. Naturally, you are one of those friends and can offer advice and support, but you do not have the power to make the alcoholic take your advice—no matter how infallible your counsel may be. Accept your powerlessness to control others, no matter how much you may love them, and start to work on trusting them—and a higher power—to take care of themselves.

DETACHMENT: PUTTING POWERLESSNESS INTO ACTION

Detachment puts the principle of powerlessness into action. Since you cannot control others, you need to give up responsibility for their behavior. You will need to learn to apply this new rule in your life, especially in relation to the alcoholic's drinking and recovery. As the first of the Twelve Steps urges, you need to recognize and accept your powerlessness over alcohol and the alcoholic. More than anything else, trying to control the uncontrollable—not just the alcoholic's drinking, but, in all likelihood, the behavior of others, too—has made your life unmanageable. If you truly want to pursue your own recovery and make your life manageable and fulfilling, you will need to detach yourself from the alcoholic's actions. Detachment signals an end to trying to fix all the problems of those you love. Now that you recognize that you have neither control over nor responsibility for the behavior of others, you need to begin to take action based on that realization.

Detaching from the problems of those you love does *not* mean that you no longer care for your loved ones. But it does shine a new light on caring, so that you look at caring from a new perspective. Detachment means caring for others without taking care of every aspect of their lives. It means caring for yourself at the same time that you care for others—not sacrificing all your own wants and needs in a futile attempt to satisfy those of another person.

Detachment embodies the philosophy of "live and let live." It allows other people to experience the effects of their own actions. Even when it hurts those you love most, you need to allow and encourage them to face up to the consequences of their behavior. If the recovering alcoholic—or someone else you love—is acting boorish at a party, for instance, you need to disavow responsibility for that behavior. Unless you detach yourself from the false sense of responsibility you feel for the behavior of others, you will never truly begin to take full responsibility for yourself. And you can stop protecting those you love from their own behavior, sooner or later they will begin to take responsibility for themselves.

Tammy, a recovering alcoholic with one year's sobriety, actually appreciates her husband's new detachment. She confesses that she had become wholly dependent on her husband's care. "When I was drinking," she explains, "Frank was very, very protective of me. I guess you could even say he was overprotective. He devoted almost every spare moment of his life to taking care of me.

"Now that I'm in AA, I don't need his protection anymore. Frankly, I've even resented it at times. But now that he's going to Al-Anon meetings, he's gradually becoming less protective. It's been a real eye-opener for him. As he sees that I can do things like take my clothes to the cleaners, pack my own lunch, and get home safely from the subway stop by myself, he's giving me the room I need to do these things on my own.

"I tell Frank that I still love it when he takes care of me, but I don't *need* him to take care of me all the time. I've had to explain to him why I need to be responsible. It makes me feel good to know that I can take care of myself."

Tammy and Frank, like most couples under the shadow of

alcoholism, had become almost totally dependent upon each other. As her alcoholism progressed, Tammy became increasingly unable to handle even the most mundane tasks. And as most codependents do, Frank stepped in to pick up the slack, doing whatever needed to be done to keep things as unruffled as possible. As Tammy became more and more helpless, Frank helped more and more. Most alcoholic relationships fall into this sort of pattern, with the alcoholic's neediness complementing the codependent's need to feel needed.

Once in sobriety, however, both people in the relationship have to figure out how to take responsibility for their individual recovery and for working on their part in the relationship. Like Tammy and Frank, you will need to find a healthy balance of responsibilities in recovery. The new, balanced sense of responsibility that grows out of your detachment will sow a vital seed for your relationship. If you continue to nurture this seed through your recovery, it will later blossom into a relationship between equal adults in a Mutual Partnership.

ESTABLISHING APPROPRIATE BOUNDARIES

In detaching yourself from the alcoholic's disease and from the problems of those you love, you will need to establish appropriate "boundaries" between yourself and others. Interpersonal boundaries are the invisible lines that separate people emotionally, making the experiences, thoughts, and feelings of one person distinct from those of another. Appropriate boundaries encourage a healthy balance between individuals and those around them. Boundaries should allow for a little give and take, remaining well defined but flexible. Appropriate family boundaries allow individual family members to remain distinct and independent yet close enough to enjoy warm, supportive relationships. For example, parents and children who have established suitable boundaries treat one another with respect and tolerance while encouraging one another's individuality. In relating to each other, family members learn to balance the complementary needs for companionship and privacy, emotional closeness and distance, attachment and disengagement. People with a secure sense of interpersonal boundaries neither get so close to others that they smother them nor remain so distant that they abandon them. They can congratulate another person's triumphs or empathize with the other's tragedies without thinking that they have to feel exactly the same way.

Whether you grew up in an alcoholic family or first became involved in an alcoholic relationship as an adult, your interpersonal boundaries have probably become blurred and imbalanced. Codependents, by definition, become overly involved in someone else's life. In the insular environment of the alcoholic household, where everyone focuses single-mindedly on the alcoholic's drinking, the line between "me" and "you" can become blurred. In most alcoholic relationships, both codependents and alcoholics end up trespassing on each other's boundaries. In all likelihood, no one in the household has set clear limits that separated appropriate and inappropriate behavior. Codependents will often go to any lengths in their attempts to please everyone around them and keep the situation "under control." But in these desperate attempts, they show little understanding of or respect for one another's boundaries. While some family members withdraw entirely from these blurred relationships, most people in alcoholic households repeatedly get in each other's way. Despite the best intentions, they usually end up violating one another's needs for privacy and individual accountability.

Often the blurring of interpersonal boundaries spills over into the arena of feelings and thoughts. Codependents begin to take on the feelings, attitudes, and opinions of the alcoholic and others in the household. When one person feels depressed or angry, codependents often feel obligated to have the identical emotion. Codependents not only accept this burden of another person's feelings, but expect others to do the same for them. "If other people really loved me," codependents tend to think, "they would feel sad when I feel blue." At the least, codependents expect others to know what they are feeling and thinking without having to bother to tell them. If your interpersonal boundaries blurred in this way, you often didn't know what you felt or where your feelings began and another's ended. The dividing line between you and those around you had gradually disintegrated.

In the earliest days of recovery, therefore, you will need to begin restructuring your relationships with those around you. If you want to move toward more balanced relationships, you will need to initiate a thorough investigation of your interpersonal boundaries. A major task of your recovery will be to establish clear boundaries in your personal relationships. But before you can do so, you need to recognize and discard the blurred ones that have contributed to the unmanageability of your life in codependency.

Ted and Janice are each recovering from both alcoholism and codependency. Both have long histories of blurred boundaries: Janice traces her boundary problems back to her childhood home, where everyone focused on her father's compulsive gambling, while Ted traces his problems to a childhood dominated by his mother's alcoholism. Together, they have worked out a system to alert each other whenever one of them starts to step across the other's personal boundary.

"Janice and I came up with the term 'my court,'" Ted explains. "It helps us define situations where either of us feels that the other is trespassing. It stops me from becoming overly involved in something that's really her business, and vice versa.

"Sometimes I feel like Janice worries too much about my problems at the office. But now, if she starts to get too upset, I just say, 'Hey Janice, you're in my court.' I don't say it rudely or anything. All I mean is that it's *my* problem and *I* can work it out. Janice doesn't need to do my worrying for me.

"Janice tells me I'm in her court whenever I take her bad moods personally. Sometimes she wakes up in a really lousy mood in the morning. Making coffee for her and trying to talk her out of her gloom almost never works anyway. So when she reminds me that I'm in her court, I back off and stop trying to get her day off to a good start. I just have to concern myself with *my* day."

Establishing clear boundaries is a lot like becoming a good doubles partner in tennis. You can offer support and encouragement and sometimes back your partner up if he or she misses a ball. But if you start "poaching"—fielding balls that your partner should return—he or she will strongly resent your interference. Neither of you will have fun. Your partner will rightly feel as if you are cutting him or her out of the game. And you will feel the unnecessary burden of trying to return every ball. Sooner or later, you will probably mis-hit a ball that your partner could have returned cleanly. You need to trust your partner to return the balls hit to his or her court. Try to relax, have some fun, and begin to enjoy the game as a team.

It takes practice for Eye-Openers to distinguish their responsibilities, actions, feelings, or attitudes from those of alcoholics. As an Eye-Opener, you will constantly need to step back and take some time to assess how emotionally connected or separated you are from your loved ones—and how close or distant you want to be. If, like Ted and Janice, you have grown too close, so you regularly trespass on each other, you will need to learn how to accept, encourage, and respect one another's space. You will need to back off a little and let other people own their feelings, thoughts, and actions. If, on the other hand, you have become too distant from others, erecting an impenetrable barrier between yourself and those around you, you will need to work on moving closer to others. Despite your initial discomfort, you will need to lower the wall, a little bit at a time, until you feel more comfortable sharing with those around you.

As with most of the tasks of recovery, establishing appropriate boundaries involves finding a delicate balance. You want to establish enough distance between yourself and others to allow yourself (and those you love) to have a distinct personality. But at the same time, you need to guard against becoming so distant from others that you end up alone. Through your new awareness and through practice, you will find this balance.

PREPARING FOR SLIPS

Most people who are new to sobriety in their relationship worry about the possibility of relapse—and rightly so. Few people succeed in breaking unhealthy habits the first time they try. No matter what the addiction, it often takes several attempts to break away from its grip. For this reason, both recovering addicts and recovering codependents must guard against the danger of a "slip"—a brief return to addictive or codependent behavior that jeopardizes their recovery and further interferes with their relationships. The alcoholic may go on a binge and start drinking again, and codependents may, as just one example, try to take over an alcoholic's recovery, forgetting their powerlessness over the other person as well as the disease.

All the major tasks that you learned in the Eye-Opener stage will be challenged if and when the alcoholic in your life suffers a relapse. If the alcoholic starts to drink again, it not only demonstrates a slip in his or her recovery, it also represents a major test of yours. You will need to call on your increasing awareness and understanding of both alcoholism and codependency to get you through this crisis. An alcoholic's relapse will challenge your success in breaking away from the obsolete, codependent, or self-destructive patterns of response on which you once relied and in trying out your new rules of behavior. It will test whether you can avoid burying the anger, depression, and grief that will follow the alcoholic's loss of sobriety. And because an alcoholic's relapse places an enormous strain on a codependent's recovery, it will put to the supreme test your new ability to accept your powerlessness over the disease, to practice detachment, and to establish appropriate boundaries.

If you can practice what you have learned as an Eye-Opener, you will manage to maintain a safe distance between your recovery and the alcoholic's and refuse to allow the alcoholic's moods to pull you down. More than anything else, you will not give the alcoholic's slip the power to cause you to relapse into codependency.

If you are ready for it, neither an alcoholic's nor a codependent's slip need lead to a full-scale relapse. Although you should avoid minimizing or excusing it, try not to think of one slip as the total failure of recovery. Even a little recovery offers people a glimmer of how much better things can be. And since you never really lose what you have truly gained, you—or the alcoholic—can recapture those good feelings and get back on the track of recovery. But it takes preparation to prevent a slip from snowballing and undermining all your recovery efforts.

Most recovering codependents spend more time worrying about the alcoholic's slips than about their own. If you share this concern, try to take care of first things first. You have no control over another person's slips, but you may be able to fight off your own. Recognizing the signs of relapse can sometime help you ward one off. Most codependents' slips and relapses are triggered by one or more of the following:

- Headaches, insomnia, or exhaustion
- Tension or mood swings
- Anger or irritability
- Depression
- Self-pity
- Isolation
- Impatience
- Failure to meet unrealistic expectations
- Overreacting or blaming
- Complacency and denial
- The use of drugs or alcohol
- Compulsive behavior (eating, shopping, gambling, and so on)
- Rationalization of self-destructive behavior
- Letting up on self-discipline

Because they are so common among codependents in the Eye-Opener stage of recovery, you may even call these triggers a codependent's "withdrawal" symptoms. Under the pressure of these stresses, recovering codependents often feel tempted to fall back on the coping methods of the past: codependent behavior. Staying alert for these signs of slipping may help stave off a relapse into codependency.

If three or more of the triggers have become a part of your everyday life, ask yourself the following two questions. Is your recovery program really working? Perhaps you need to find new meetings, get a sponsor, seek professional help if you aren't already getting it, or seek a different kind of professional help if you are. And are you really working at your recovery program? Maybe you need to attend more meetings; talk to your sponsor more frequently; and talk to friends, other people in the program, and professionals about your fears of relapse.

Once you're convinced that you're doing everything you can to prevent your slips, then you can turn your attention to making plans for the alcoholic's. Like codependents, alcoholics experience psychological withdrawal symptoms that can signal a relapse. But alcoholics also suffer from physical withdrawal. The addict's recovery from alcoholism or another addiction involves profound physical changes that invariably exact a heavy toll. If a relative, lover, or friend has fewer than ninety days of sobriety, you can expect your loved one to experience some of the following symptoms of withdrawal:

- Tingling body sensations and physical numbness
- Muscle pains or spasms
- Tremors, shakiness, and headaches
- Loss of appetite or stomach problems or both
- Insomnia or exhaustion or both
- Sexual difficulties (performance anxiety, impotence, lack of physical desire, and so on)
- Blurred vision
- Extreme sensitivity to noise, light, taste, smell, and touch
- Memory loss and confusion

The body repairs gradually, so some of these problems may persist even longer than ninety days. As Tim, a recovering alcoholic who sees me for therapy, acknowledges, "I was exhausted for thirteen months!" Unfortunately, knowing that withdrawal is common will neither make these symptoms go away nor make them easier to cope with. And these physical stresses cannot help but affect the newly sober alcoholic's nervous system and emotional and mental health.

"I'm always afraid Stuart might start drinking again. He insists on doing it his own way without the AA program," complains Terry, whose husband has not taken a drink for four months. "And as far as I can see, there's no big difference. It's like he's been freeze-dried. He's not drinking, but his behavior and attitudes are still the same. He's just as arrogant, miserable, nasty to everyone, and totally self-centered as he ever was."

Terry's husband Stuart is suffering from the "dry-drunk" syndrome—mental and emotional withdrawal symptoms that mimic alcoholic behavior. In many ways, these attitudes and feelings parallel the codependent's "withdrawal" symptoms. Common signs of dry-drunk behavior include the following:

- Low self-esteem
- Fluctuating moods
- Depression and irritability
- Nervousness and anxiety
- A low tolerance for stress or frustration of any kind
- Living in the past or future, instead of the present
- Self-centeredness
- Distrust or blame of others
- Isolation and lack of communication

Further into recovery, the dry-drunk syndrome and the alcoholic's physical withdrawal symptoms will begin to fade. But until then, either physical or psychological withdrawal can trigger an alcoholic's slips and relapses. Almost everyone—addict and nonaddict alike—has some "bad days," when he or she will exhibit many of the attitudes just listed. But in many cases, these symptoms will worsen just before either a brief slip or a long-term relapse drags the alcoholic back into the disease. "I felt better before, when I was still drinking" can be a pretty good excuse to pick up a drink—especially if the alcoholic is looking for some sort of justification. So if the alcoholic begins to experience more than a few of these "bad days" in a row, take some precautions to protect yourself and your recovery.

You cannot do anything to control whether a recovering alcoholic slips back into alcoholism or addiction. All you can do is tell the alcoholic what you have observed and communicate your concern, urge her or him to get help, and then wipe your hands of it. The biggest danger in a recovering relationship, however, is that the alcoholic's slips can trigger your slips —and vice versa—and plunge you both back into the abyss of disease. But if you have begun to construct appropriate personal boundaries and can practice detachment, the alcoholic's slip need not have a negative impact on your personal recovery. Since you cannot control each other's recovery, you need to do everything you can to prevent one person's slip from setting this vicious cycle in motion.

Since lapses in recovery can sometimes catch you off guard, it's wise to discuss with the alcoholic *in advance* what you will do if either of you slips. Regard slips as possible emergencies or crises for which you had better be prepared. They may never happen. But just as you should plan escape routes in your home, so you will be prepared *just in case* of a fire, you need to come up with a plan that you will automatically put into action in case of a slip. Knowing that you have a plan of action will allow you to relax, and let what happens happen. Terry, who earlier described her husband's dry-drunk symptoms, has not yet developed a plan to cope with relapse; therefore, she constantly worries about it. But if you and the alcoholic each come up with a plan for dealing with slips—and share your plans with each other—then you won't have to become obsessive about the possibility of this emergency. You'll know you can handle it if and when it occurs.

What sort of plan should you have to deal with the alcoholic's or your slips and prevent them from leading to a long-term relapse for both of you? Your plan should include all actions that will best protect you and other members of your family, especially children. It should leave no room for ambiguity for either of you, so you can automatically put it into effect during the extremely stressful time that comes in the wake of a slip. Most important, though, you must be fully willing to follow through with this plan and then communicate this commitment to the alcoholic. Each of you needs to know in no uncertain terms that any slip or relapse will bring immediate and concrete consequences.

At my urging, Lois worked out a plan to handle slips that she then shared with her husband in one of our couples counseling sessions. Holding Vince's hands in hers, Lois looked directly into his eyes and told him, "If you start to drink again, I'm going to take the kids and move out. And we'll stay away until I know from your sponsor that you are dry and going to meetings every day. When you have put two straight weeks of sobriety together, then we'll come back.

"I hope you understand my need to protect myself and the children. This isn't a threat, but we need to have a plan for ourselves. It's not good for any of us to be living in a house with an active alcoholic. I honestly hope this won't happen, and I truly believe you can stay sober if you continue to work your program. But I don't want to take the chance of falling backwards. We've all come a long way already, and I just want to keep moving forward."

Vince and Lois both cried and hugged each other when she finished relating her plan. To Vince's credit, he did not react defensively and agreed that she needed to prepare for this possible emergency. Six months later, Lois and Vince have still not had to resort to this plan. But they can both rest easier knowing that they have prepared this "insurance policy."

In preparing your own emergency plan, keep the following guidelines in mind:

1. Keep the focus on yourself and *your* recovery. Remember that this is your primary rule of the Eye-Opener stage.
2. Your own recovery matters, no matter what the addict does.
3. Don't try to rescue. Ask someone for help—for yourself as well as for the recovering alcoholic.
4. Tell the addict that you expect her or him to treat any slip as a medical emergency. Let the addict know that you expect her or him to try recovery again, even after a slip.
5. Know your own bottom line before you get to it. State it and stick to it.
6. Renew your own commitment to recovery. Keep making positive changes in your life.

If you can follow these guidelines, you will come up with a reasonable and appropriate response to the alcoholic's slips or relapses.

Try not to judge yourself as harsh, insensitive, or selfish because you have developed this essential escape route just for yourself. Having a plan will not undercut the alcoholic's recovery. If he or she truly wants to recover, a contingency plan will reinforce that commitment; the alcoholic will gain the added motivation of avoiding these dire consequences. You can still be as supportive of the alcoholic's recovery as you feel you can. But you can't do yourself—or anyone else—any good if you allow the alcoholic's slips to drag you back into the darkness. And that's exactly what these plans are designed to prevent.

Just because you have a plan, though, does not mean you can afford to be overly confident. The recovering alcoholic's slip or relapse will bring on a rush of emotions that may catch you off guard. Plan or no plan, you will certainly feel angry, embarrassed, disappointed, and hurt. Your continued involvement in your own recovery program can help you deal with these feelings. People who are involved in AA and Al-Anon know all the signs of slips and their aftereffects. Since old-timers in recovery programs know what you can and cannot expect in the Eye-Opener stage of recovery, they can help alert you to signs of slips and keep you on track. And when you or the alcoholic run into one of these rough spots of recovery, people in self-help programs can provide you with much-needed reassurance and good advice.

If it happens, try to consider a slip—or even a long-term relapse—as a lesson that teaches you to keep trying instead of giving up. Each slip offers you a new opportunity to learn more about yourself and the alcoholic—although, it is hoped, neither of you will require too many of these hard lessons. Should a slip occur, the first priority for each of you is to maintain or get back to your own recovery. Once you have *both* accomplished this goal, try to review with each other the actions that may have led up to this slip. If you work together to develop an understanding of lapses, you can take steps to prevent history from repeating itself. At the same time, you will renew your commitment to your personal growth and the growth of your relationship.

PART II

The
Pioneer
Stage

3

<u>S</u>ELF-<u>D</u>ISCOVERY

In the Eye-Opener stage, you concentrated primarily on *stopping* old codependent behaviors—denial, enabling, rescuing, controlling—that had kept you locked into illness. Instead, you started to take charge of your life, becoming more aware, active, and assertive. You made a commitment not to shut your eyes to the problems of addiction and codependency anymore. For perhaps the first time in your life, you began to talk, trust, and feel. You began to establish more appropriate boundaries between yourself and others, detaching yourself from their problems and letting go of your desire to control every aspect of your life—and of the lives of those around you. You recognized some of the unhealthy patterns in your life and started to break away from them. As you let go of your links to codependency, you will naturally move on to the Pioneer stage of recovery.

As Pioneers, you and the sober alcoholic will each need to embark on individual journeys of self-discovery. This pioneering journey will not only increase your awareness and acceptance of yourself, but will help eliminate one of the most common resentments of couples in recovery. Many codependents in the Pioneer stage complain that alcoholics become "overinvolved" with their own recovery program—that recovering alcoholics are just as "absent" as are active alcoholics. If you share this kind of resentment, try to concentrate on your individual recovery for the time being. By becoming involved in your own life instead of continuing to focus on the alcoholic's, you will build a firm foundation for relationship recovery.

Do you have to be by yourself while focusing on yourself? By no means. Although this journey of self-discovery must, by definition, be taken by you alone, you don't have to feel lonely as a Pioneer. As you explore the new territory of yourself, rely on the support of those involved in your recovery program. Think of the other members of your Al-Anon or other self-help group, your therapist, or any other supporters as outposts along your journey. Al-Anon members, in particular, because they have traveled this territory before, can offer you valuable guidance and support. So you would be wise to stop at one of these Pioneer outposts whenever you feel tired, frustrated, or lost during your journey. Each can offer you comfort, sustenance, and direction that will help keep you on the right trail.

You may wonder whether you have to put all relationships on hold until you discover everything you need to learn about yourself. Certainly not. Alcoholism and codependency, the co-conspirators of this family disease, have isolated you for too long already. You should certainly make an effort to improve relationships—through your increased honesty, openness, and understanding of yourself and others. But for now, your first priority in recovery needs to be yourself. The more secure sense of self you develop through recovery, the better your chances are for improved relationships. So, for perhaps the first time in your life, you will need to put yourself first.

"My number one priority is taking care of myself in recovoery," acknowledges Ben, who admits that he doesn't know how much his relationship can improve right now. "Just because Zoe has been sober for four months doesn't mean our relationship is fine. Since I started going to Al-Anon a year ago, we're at very different places in recovery and I can't change that.

"I think I'm becoming a lot less protective of Zoe, but she still expects the protection. All I can do is encourage her to go to meetings and talk to her sponsor. And that's what I have to do for myself, too. I think she understands now why I have to work on my program by myself and she has to work on hers. We both know that later we'll have a lot of work to do on our relationship. But I'm convinced we can't have much of a relationship until we both have some solid recovery."

Ben recognizes that the recovery of his relationship depends first on his personal recovery. Although he can provide Zoe with love and understanding, he cannot live for her or solve her problems anymore. He needs to begin with the one thing under his control: his recovery. He had made a commitment to himself to try to understand and accept the person he is today. This awareness and self-acceptance will provide the basis for better relationships today and tomorrow.

Your journey of self-discovery, like Ben's, will prove essential not only to your recovery, but to the recovery of your relationships. By becoming the person you've always wanted to be, you will begin to move toward the kind of relationships you've always hoped for. Even though you (and the alcoholic) may not be actively working on improving your relationships, by learning how to care for yourself, you will actually become better able to care for others. You will need to look at where you are now and where you want to go. If you don't know these things, you cannot possibly communicate them to the recovering alcoholic—or to anyone else. Through your work as a Pioneer, though, you will develop a solid sense of yourself. And you can carry this new awareness and confidence into all your relationships. So whether you ultimately decide to stay in a relationship with the alcoholic in your life or build new relationships with other people, you will need to undertake this critical journey of self-discovery.

WHO ARE YOU NOW?

In the Eye-Opener stage, you recognized your codependency and decided that you didn't want to be codependent anymore. But if you are no longer a codependent, who are you? You may have spent years looking after other people—not just in your current relationship, but probably in your childhood as well. If you are like most recovering codependents, though, you rarely looked after yourself—or at yourself. You were probably much too wrapped up in other people's lives to spend much time wondering about your own identity, your needs, and your desires.

Now that you have decided to live your own life instead of trying to manage other people's, you need to look at who you are and what you want from life in recovery. The process of self-discovery you will undertake as a Pioneer demands more than mere self-examination. Simply *knowing* what you're feeling, thinking, and doing in your day-to-day life will not be enough. You will need to *question* your emotions, thoughts, and actions with a critical eye, continually challenging them to see whether they will get you where you want to go. To shift your perspective inward instead of outward and get started in the critical task of self-discovery, you may find it helpful to ask yourself some of the following questions about what you're *feeling, thinking,* and *doing.*

Do you feel anything? Even after the eye-opening rush of emotions in the first months of recovery, Pioneers often feel numb. After repressing your feelings for so long, you may not be used to having them. You may feel so uncomfortable with your emotions that you continue to push them below the surface. In your early days as a Pioneer in recovery, you may have to train yourself to dig a little deeper. Do whatever you can to dredge up your feelings and bring them into your consciousness.

"Getting to my feelings is by no means automatic," admits Grant, a thirty-eight-year-old addictions counselor who started marital counseling with his wife six months ago. "After so many years of practice, it would be easy for me to just deny my feelings and go on with something else. But I realize now that I have to go through a whole routine if I want to bring my feelings out into the open at last. I'm not even sure what they are most of the time, so first I have to take the time to think about them.

"Whenever other people put me on the spot and want to know what I'm feeling about something, I try to give myself a little time. My old way was to respond automatically with what I thought they wanted to hear, not what I really felt. But now I say, 'I'm not sure, let me think about it for a few minutes.' That way, I buy myself time to figure out what I feel before I answer. And I take all the time I need to allow my feelings to come up."

Like Grant, you may need to put some time and effort into the task of discovering your present feelings. If long-buried feelings from the past are still interfering with today's feelings, you may need to explore these old feelings before you can move past them. In addition, you may want to try to develop a routine to keep in touch with your emotions on a day-to-day basis. Through habitual effort, you can condition yourself to feel your feelings regularly and spontaneously.

Do you share your feelings with anyone? When you were living with an active alcoholic, even when you knew what you felt, you probably didn't dare express it. Codependents often live in fear that almost any remark may set off an alcoholic's drinking—or even worse. In an atmosphere in which verbal or physical violence may erupt at any instant, it is unsafe to express feelings. If you lived in this kind of environment, you probably seldom risked talking, especially about personal feelings—which the alcoholic might have ignored or even used as ammunition against you in a later argument.

Pioneers in recovery need to find safe places to share feelings. Most Pioneers begin opening up about their emotions in the rooms of self-help meetings or in the offices of their therapists. But once you've taken the risk in these safe environments, you will find it easier to express your feelings in the course of your day-to-day life.

"I'm starting to notice a change in the way I talk to people now," observes Beth, a twenty-five-year-old divorcée whose ex-husband, father, and two brothers are all alcoholics. "It used to be that all I could talk about were impersonal things—the weather; the latest movie I saw; and maybe, just maybe, what I was doing at work. If I was talking with someone in my family, at the end of a phone call I might say, '. . . and how are you?' But I don't think I ever really meant it. And I certainly never expected anyone to answer by actually talking about their feelings. You just didn't do that in our family. We were too busy trying to look like the perfect family to admit to any feelings.

"Now that I'm no longer in denial, I can see my family as it really is. And with the practice I'm getting in Al-Anon and in my therapy sessions, I'm starting to ask about other people's feelings and to share mine. It's a new and slow process. But there are occasional breakthroughs, and I can really tell I'm changing. The other night I telephoned my brother Ron—he's in a recovery program, too, now—and I actually started out the conversation by asking how he was feeling. And this time, I really wanted to know and he really told me. It was probably the most honest conversation—heck, the *first* honest conversation—we've ever had in our whole lives."

Recovery makes it safe to talk about the F-word: feelings. You will feel better and more confident in yourself when you can finally open up and be honest with other people.

Do you think you're being "selfish" in concentrating on yourself during the Pioneer stage? As a codependent, you spent too many years self*less*ly giving up your life for the sake of others. Now, if you want to get better, you need to concentrate your energy and attention on yourself. Since this requires a little selfishness, for once in your life, give yourself permission to give yourself what you need. It's okay.

"Recovery *is* selfish," acknowledges Cathy, a twenty-eight-year-old high school teacher. "The only life I am capable of saving is my own. And to do that I need to think about me. It's a new experience for me, after ten years of trying to save Peter from his disease. But now that we both have individual recovery programs, we know we have to work our own programs if we're ever going to have a good life together. Our recovery, and our relationship, depends upon our selfishness at this point in our lives."

A long-overdue period of self-care at this stage of your recovery does not mean that you've become a selfish person for good or that you will always have to be selfish in relating to your loved ones. Don't worry. It's not in your personality to be selfish all the time. Try to think of this period of "selfish" concentration on your recovery as an adjustment, rather than as a total overhaul. You can still be the giving person you've always been; you'll just have to give more to yourself, instead of giving everything to the other people in your life.

Do you think, "This time will be different"? You've probably had this optimistic thought hundreds of times before, only to see it disintegrate into yet another disappointment. Indeed, things probably got worse instead of better with each new false expectation. But this time *can* and *will* be different. If both you and the alcoholic are in recovery—or even if the alcoholic drops out—things will get better because *you* will be changing. There is no guarantee that your relationship will fully recover. But because you had the courage to risk recovery, *you* will improve. And as you change your behavior and attitudes toward your relationships, your relationships will invariably improve, too.

Do you think you're taking only "baby steps" toward your recovery? Sometimes Pioneers want to move forward by giant leaps. They want to jump straight to the end of recovery, skipping the long process of reaching inward and outward. But this slower process is what recovery is all about. "Quick fixes" don't work any better in recovery than they did in addiction. If you have patience, deliberation, motivation, and commitment, those tentative baby steps will eventually become surefooted strides. If you maintain a slow and steady pace, you will ultimately get where you want to go.

Do you do more for yourself and less for others now? If you find that you are still minding someone else's business, remind yourself that whatever anyone else feels or thinks or does is *not* your business. Focus on yourself and make recovery your main business.

Try to do special things just for yourself and your enjoyment. What activity gives you the most pleasure during the course of your day-to-day life? It may be something as simple as quiet time, when you "do" nothing. How many minutes or hours a day do you allow yourself to spend doing that activity? Every day for a week, add five more minutes for that pleasurable activity. Then, over the course of the next month, maintain that extra half hour a day for your activity. At the end of the month, reevaluate whether you've given yourself sufficient time for pleasure or whether you need to add more time. Please, no subtractions.

Do you try to do too much and then judge yourself harshly because you've failed to meet your unrealistic expectations? Even in recovery, codependents often feel they "should" be doing more or recovering faster. If you put too much pressure on yourself, you may want to trace this feeling back to its roots. In many cases, this sense that "I'm never enough" reaches all the way back to childhood in an alcoholic home. Even if you did not grow up in an alcoholic home, your sense of inadequacy probably sprang from failed efforts to do the impossible: to control someone else's out-of-control behavior. In any addictive relationship, both children and adults think it's all their fault when other codependents remain depressed or the addict falls off the wagon. Mistakenly believing that if they only behaved "better," the situation in the home would improve, family members constantly chastise themselves for failing in these efforts. All too often, this overly harsh critique of themselves continues throughout the early stages of relationship recovery.

In trying to be the *perfect* recovering person, you will quickly become your own worst enemy. If you have sincerely dedicated yourself to your recovery and do the best you can each day, you are doing enough. If you still judge yourself too harshly, you may not be capable of saying you are doing the best you can. If so, you need a daily reminder. Make a little card and tape it to your bathroom mirror. Print: "I *am* enough. I'm doing the best I can today. That's all I *can* do and that *is* enough." Make sure to read this declaration of self-worth each time you look in the mirror. And look in the mirror often. Looking at yourself is the whole idea of the Pioneer stage.

Do you make mistakes? Good! If you can answer yes to this question and admit to your mistakes, then you've made significant progress in your personal recovery. In trying to be perfect while coping with the addict's illness, chances are that you didn't allow yourself to make any mistakes, or at least any you'd admit. You may have even enjoyed always being right. Perhaps you needed a sense of self-righteousness to bolster your self-esteem, to shore up the unsteady part of yourself that constantly felt pummeled by the disease. But now that you are getting wiser and stronger every day, you no longer need to hold on to that self-righteousness. After all, underneath it all, you never really believed it yourself. As a Pioneer, you'll know that you don't have to be right all the time. Sure, you'll make plenty of mistakes and you won't always feel comfortable with imperfection. But, it is hoped, you'll learn something from most of your mistakes.

WHERE DO YOU WANT TO GO?

Although you may not know exactly where recovery will lead, rest assured you've started out in the right direction. You know you *don't* want to go back to the misery, depression, doubt, chaos, inconsistency, confusion, humiliation, embarrassment, and shame that went along with addiction and co-dependency. However, you should not completely shut the door on your past. It's helpful to remember what that person you once were was like and what your life was like then. By remembering the past, you can guard against falling into old patterns of being and behaving.

Like many Pioneers, you may want to know exactly where recovery will take you. Unfortunately, no one can know what will happen tomorrow. So try to become more comfortable with the uncertainty of the future, with the fact that you're involved in a transition from illness to recovery. Try not to allow your expectations to become unreasonably high or unambitiously low. If you can temper your optimism with some reasonable doubts and push past your doubts with some well-warranted optimism, you will make your way through recovery. Remind yourself that you don't need to know where you're going every step of the way.

Why should you know where recovery will lead you? Everything about recovery is new to you: you have entered unexplored territory, which may at first seem strange and ominous. You may not yet feel comfortable with this new state of emotional sobriety, and recovery may seem tenuous. But you have already demonstrated your courage and willingness to change by choosing the unmapped territory of recovery. Now you need to continue moving forward, charting your course as you go along. As long as you're moving away from the codependency of the past toward the promises of the present and the future, you'll know you're heading the right way.

What promises do you hope recovery will fulfill? The "Big Book" of Alcoholics Anonymous, used by recovering alcoholics and often helpful to members of other Twelve-Step programs, states that recovery promises the following:

We are going to know a new freedom and a new happiness. . . .
We will comprehend the word serenity and we will know peace.
No matter how far down the scale we have gone, we will see
how our experience can benefit others. That feeling of useless-
ness and self-pity will disappear. . . . Our whole attitude and
outlook upon life will change. . . . We will intuitively know how
to handle situations which used to baffle us. . . .

Are these extravagant promises? We think not. They are being
fulfilled among us—sometimes quickly, sometimes slowly. They
will always materialize if we work for them.

Are any of these promises becoming a part of your life and relationships in recovery? Be grateful for those that have already come true or that seem to be coming true now. And set those that you haven't yet realized as your goals for the future. What other promises would you add as further goals for your recovery? Write down the promises you are willing to make to yourself in the course of your recovery. Can you keep them? Or have you tried to promise something that's either out of your control or beyond your reach?

As you continue on your Pioneering journey of self-discovery, remember that your expectations, hopes, and dreams are just as much a part of your identity as are your feelings, thoughts, and behavior. Explore your dreams as well as your reality. Write down some of the things you hope to achieve or accomplish in your recovery. Don't bother to make an exhaustive list. As you change, your goals may change as well; so tomorrow's list may be different. What are some of the goals you have set for yourself? Your relationships? Share your list with your recovery group or your therapist. They'll let you know if they think you're being realistic. But remember, even if others say you're being unrealistic, if a particular goal is important enough to you and you honestly think you can achieve it, don't let anyone dissuade you from it. You're entitled to your dreams.

VALUING YOURSELF

At this point in your recovery, you may not believe that you are entitled to your dreams. For that matter, you may not believe you are entitled to anything. After years of living in the shadow of addiction, you may have gotten in the practice of minimizing your value. But no matter what you once thought, you are entitled to yourself, your recovery, and your dreams.

"The entire time I was involved with my alcoholic partner, I felt unvalued or undervalued by him. Obviously, I didn't value myself either," adds Janet, a music teacher, whose attitude has changed dramatically in recovery, "or I wouldn't have stayed in that sick situation for fifteen years. But I'm not going to blame myself. I stayed because at that time, I couldn't leave. I just didn't know how.

"Shortly after I got into the Al-Anon program, though, I started to feel I deserved my recovery. I knew I had a long way to go to become the whole person I wanted to be, but I knew I was important. And now that I've finally discovered how important I am, I'm 'showing up for life'—that's an Al-Anon slogan. I *am* showing up for life—my life."

Of all the new values you will need to define in recovery, the most important is the value of yourself. In the past, you probably devalued yourself as you inflated the alcoholic's importance. You may never have developed a secure sense of who you are. As a Pioneer, however, you will develop a stronger understanding of yourself and what you want. But to accomplish this goal, you must believe in your own importance. You have to know that you matter.

Believing in yourself and your right to recovery is a powerful statement of entitlement. If you are like most Pioneers, though, you may need an occasional push before you will claim all your entitlements—in other words, before you demand what is rightfully yours: your identity, your recovery, happiness, a better life. Since addiction generates low self-esteem among all those who are touched by it, codependents often feel unsure whether they are entitled to anything other than what they've got. If you don't always feel one hundred percent certain that you deserve a better life, you may find it helpful to repeat the following statements of entitlement every day:

> I'm entitled to my self.
> I'm entitled to my recovery.
> I'm entitled to get help in my recovery.
> I'm entitled to all my feelings.

If you don't feel you deserve to get better, say these statements out loud every day. If you continue to have trouble, say them even louder. A forceful voice is sometimes needed to convince that person in the mirror.

As Janet discovered, placing a value on yourself starts a whole process of establishing other values that prove self-promoting rather than self-defeating. Simply wanting to change and seeking recovery demonstrate that you believe your life is worth saving—even if you can't save the life of anyone else you love. In desiring recovery, therefore, you've already made a strong start to move toward self-worth. In itself, this belief in your own importance will begin to transform your life. A long series of positive attitudes and changed behaviors will develop from your acceptance of your basic right to be the center of your life. And these new attitudes and behaviors will allow you to redefine yourself, to become the new person you've always wanted to be.

NEW IDENTITIES, CHANGING ROLES

As Pioneers begin to form a better sense of who they are and what they want, they find new, more comfortable, and more satisfying ways of being in the world. And this means finding new roles for themselves in all their relationships—inside and outside the home. People tend to play certain roles in their relationships—most often roles carried over from their childhood into their adult lives. As a child, you probably played a particular role in your family. Do you still play this role in your current relationships? Does it help or hinder your present relationships, especially the one with the recovering alcoholic?

If you want to discard old roles and cast yourself in new ones in recovery, it is important to be aware of the roles you have played in the past and those you now play. Examine the list of unbalanced family and relationship roles that follows. Place a check next to the roles you have played in the past, and circle the roles you play (or still play) today.

UNBALANCED FAMILY ROLES

Caretaker	Goody Two-Shoes
Care Receiver	Black Sheep
Victim	Superhero
Bully	Scapegoat
Perfect Person	Stoical Martyr
Lost Cause	Endless Whiner
Dudley Do Right	Hermit
Dudley Do Wrong	Clinging Vine
Favorite	Manager
Unloved	Managed
Know-Nothing	Grown-Up Before Your Time
Know-It-All	Baby of the Family
Attention Grabber	Serious Sobersides
Invisible Child	Frivolous Frolicker
Controller	Fearless Leader
Controlled	Fearful Follower
Worrier	Enabler/Helper
Apathetic One	Enabled/Helpless
Rescuer	Peacemaker
Rescued	Troublemaker

In looking at yourself and your roles, you may find it helpful to place yourself in relation to other family members or other people who are or have been close to you. Write in the names of close friends or family members who star (or starred) in these roles, too. How did your role complement or play off their roles? Did your role change, depending on which person you were with and what the person expected of you?

In recovery, you no longer need to try to be the person whom the alcoholic and the other people in your life wanted you to be. If, as an Eye-Opener, you have already discarded your old codependent role, as a Pioneer, you now have to try on new roles until you find the ones that fit the true you. You may want to think about giving up some roles, toning down others, and even engaging in trial periods of role reversals with the recovering alcoholic. Guard against falling back into your childhood roles or any unbalanced, rigidly patterned relationships.

If you tend to be the "household manager" in your current relationship, for instance, you may ask the alcoholic to take over the bill paying for a few months. Or you may approach the recovering alcoholic and say something like, "I really hate paying all the bills month after month. Let's try sitting down once a month for an hour or so and getting them done together. I'm sure that will make me less angry about it. Not only that, but it will also give you a more realistic idea about what I mean when I say we cannot afford a car this year." By experimenting with shared responsibilities, you will be ready to move to Mutual Partnerships.

Like so much of recovery, the new roles you need to discover for yourself involve finding a balance—not displaying too much or too little of any one quality. In the past, you may have tended toward extremes. In an atmosphere of illness, for example, some codependents become inflexible in trying to control the mess of addiction. In sobriety, rigid codependents must try to become more flexible, while not abandoning all personal rules, regulations, and structure. Or, like many recovering codependents, you may have difficulty finding a balance between the extremes of grandiosity and self-negation. In addictive relationships, alcoholics and codependents tend to move to opposite ends of this scale, so that one person is always on top and the other is always on the bottom. During the Pioneer stage, the grandiose person has to learn more humility and have his or her ego deflated a notch or two, while the insecure person needs to gain more self-confidence and practice self-assertion. When both people begin to feel centered or balanced, then they can move toward each other in new ways.

In trying new roles, think of yourself as a tightrope walker.

If you feel yourself reeling too far in one direction, make every effort to pull yourself in the other direction, even if it feels like you're pulling too far at first. Finding the right balance involves constant adjustments, pulling back from certain tendencies that will upset your equilibrium and pushing forward toward their opposites.

It may take you a little time to find this kind of balance in your new life. No one ever feels completely comfortable in a new role, so try not to expect miracles to happen overnight. At first, you may feel lost without your old familiar role to fall back on. So try to be patient with yourself—and with the recovering alcoholic, who will be trying new roles as well. Allow yourself and the alcoholic some time to adjust to the new roles you play in all your various relationships.

"I have to stop myself at least ten times a day from calling home to check up on Phyllis," confesses Ed, a banking executive who describes himself as his family's "chief worrier" and "superdad." "I just don't trust that she'll take care of all those things she never took care of when she was drunk. I worry about things like will she take the meat out of the freezer, make the kids' dental appointments, pick up the cat at the vet's. . . .

"I don't know how to stop worrying. I even wrote a big note to myself that says, 'Let it be,' and pasted it to my telephone. Well, that's easier said than done. My Al-Anon sponsor tells me *my feelings are legitimate, but my actions aren't*. And he's right. I can worry all I want and I have a right to be concerned, but Phyllis *is* taking care of things on the homefront and as long as she does, I have to stay off her turf."

Ed feels understandably lost, having given up his old familiar and satisfying roles in the family. He no longer has to be superdad and chief worrier, but he hasn't yet figured out who he wants to be. In an individual counseling session, Ed told me that he'd been in the driver's seat for so long that he didn't feel comfortable in the backseat as far as his family was concerned. He understands that Phyllis needs to take a more active and competent role in the family to overcome her guilt and defensiveness over her alcoholic absences. But like many codependents, Ed deeply resents Phyllis's newly responsible role. He told me he feels "left out" of the family's day-to-day affairs.

Although he certainly has to give up some of his power in the family, Ed pulled back too far, overcompensating in trying to strike a new balance. He can still find new ways to feel responsible and appreciated in his family. But I advised him that to do so, he needs to share his feelings about their shifting roles with Phyllis as well as with me. If both of them can admit their fears and resentments to each other, they can move toward a more balanced arrangement. In adopting an unequal family arrangement, Ed feels cheated and Phyllis may feel overwhelmed. But by working together, they can probably come up with a more egalitarian and sharing approach to parenting and living together as a family. They can begin to look upon their parenting as a mutual responsibility, instead of something in the exclusive domain of just one parent.

If you have children, they may need a little help adjusting to your changing roles as parents and to their shifting roles in recovery. Without some guidance, children seldom understand their parents' recovery process. Parents need to bring their children into the recovery process, providing them with as much information about addiction and recovery as they can absorb at their age. What is just as important, or even more important, than knowledge, however, is that parents need to provide their children with strong encouragement to talk about their feelings honestly. Like their father, for example, Ed and Phyllis's children may not trust the recovering alcoholic in her newly responsible role. But if they feel they can openly discuss this distrust, probably for the first time in their lives, then they can work together as a family to overcome it.

Children may also need help discovering new, more appropriate roles for themselves. When alcoholic and codependent parents are emotionally or physically absent, children take on specialized roles in a family—childhood roles that often lie at the root of adult codependency. Sharon Wegscheider-Cruse, author of *Another Chance: Hope and Health for the Alcoholic Family,* has identified these roles as the following: family hero, scapegoat, lost child, and mascot. When you change, your children will need to change, too. In giving up their old roles, children—like adults—experience a sense of loss. They also will need to mourn their loss. Recovering parents need to give their children permission to feel whatever they feel and encourage them to express these turbulent emotions.

In a later couples session, Ed and Phyllis both confided that they feel they haven't been good parents. I tried to reassure them that people are not born either "good" or "bad" parents. Anyone who is willing to work on self-improvement can become a better parent in recovery. Like any other role, the parts of "father" and "mother" will probably demand some trial and error and some adjustments before Ed and Phyllis feel comfortable with them. In shaping new roles for each family member, I encouraged the family to work on the following:

- Encourage children, through words and examples, to talk about their feelings.
- Think about the role each child played in the addictive environment. Think about what giving up an old role may mean to children. Try to help each child feel "special" in a more appropriate way (without resorting to budding codependency).
- Be consistent and calm in setting limits and rules during this period of adjustment for the family as a whole and for all its members. Establish rules that allow for some flexibility.
- Try not to overreact when children break rules. In establishing new rules and new roles, parents and children need to negotiate and renegotiate. Patience and tolerance are essential.

As each of you discovers who you really are, you will assume and discard a great variety of new roles in your relationship and in your family. Trying out new roles can be fun as well as challenging. If you remind yourself that you can always reverse a role if you don't like it, you'll have more fun with these "auditions." Remember to allow enough time to get used to these new roles. What feels uncomfortable today may feel a little more comfortable tomorrow. By rehearsing several different roles, you will eventually find the one or ones that best fit who you are now and who you want to be.

What role would you like to play now that you know yourself better as a Pioneer? Do you think you can discuss with the recovering alcoholic the roles you'd both like to play and the feelings that come with losing an old role and adopting a new one? Can you ask the alcoholic to play a supporting role as you practice your new one? Can you return the favor?

Jack and Verna, married for twenty-four years, got into recovery programs just nine months ago. In a couples counseling session, I encouraged them to share with each other what they want from their relationship in sobriety. Jack listed his three most important desires as the ability to communicate openly, an uncluttered home, and the discovery of mutual interests. Verna wanted increased understanding of her addiction, a listening ear, and more time together. In spelling out their needs to each other, Jack and Verna discovered, much to their astonishment, that what each wanted complemented the other's desires. Knowing what the other person valued, Verna and Jack sensitized themselves to each other's needs and tried to fulfill these needs as best they could. In this way, they were better able to play supporting roles in their recovering relationship.

PRACTICE, PRACTICE, PRACTICE

Self-discovery involves more than simply asking who you are. You need to know where you want to go, recognize your own importance, and try new roles until you find those that fit you best. All these actions will contribute to your growing self-awareness and self-acceptance, but lasting change—a new definition of yourself and your identity—demands action as well. To reinforce your sense that you are a new person in a new situation—a recovering person in the process of getting better —you will have to take the risk of acting in new ways. These three principles—awareness, acceptance, and action—are what Al-Anon recommends as the foundation on which you can build a sober life.

Taking chances, making choices, and acting upon them often sound like a tall order to most Pioneers. Knowing and accepting that they have options doesn't make it any easier for Pioneers—or anyone else—to take immediate action and choose one. But try not to let fear intimidate you from acting. If you swallow hard and "act as if," you can learn to overcome your fear.

In recovery, people often need to act as if. This kind of "personal brainwashing" can help people change even when they feel most incapable of change. If you want to act as if, all you have to do is pretend you can do something and then just do it—no matter how persistently the little voice inside your head says you can't. If you try this strategy, you'll probably surprise yourself: You'll discover that you really could do it all along. Although you may have felt unsure of yourself, you will discover that you have a great many strengths you may never have suspected. By acting as if you can and doing the very thing you fear the most, you will eradicate your fear.

Acting as if can work in any situation that makes you feel afraid or uncertain of yourself. You may not believe this strategy will work. But act as if it will work anyway. And it will!

- If you feel unsure about yourself on a new job, act as if you're confident. In doing the job, you will actually become confident.
- If you doubt your ability to speak up at a particular meeting, act as if you can do it anyway. You'll speak up and prove to yourself that you have the ability.
- If you know you want to stop trying to rescue other people in your life but you're not sure whether you can, act as if you know that you can stop. You'll stop rescuing people and redefine yourself in the process.

Pioneers often feel afraid to go any further in recovery. But by learning to act as if, they prove their courage to themselves over and over again. In most cases, acting as if becomes a self-fulfilling prophecy.

Acting as if can be a powerful expression of your courage. Unlike denial, which springs from fear, acting as if is a helpful and healthy kind of pretending because it will keep you moving forward instead of sliding backward.

PERSONAL AFFIRMATIONS

Reminding yourself of your potential and your progress toward realizing that potential can strengthen and accelerate the positive transformation brought about by recovery. Many Pioneers find it helpful and encouraging to list their most positive thoughts and feelings about themselves. Writing down your self-affirmations—a series of sentences that begin with "I am . . ." or "I can . . ."—will help you feel better about yourself. And you can channel these good feelings into producing even more positive and life-affirming changes.

To get started, you (and the recovering alcoholic) can use the following list of "Happy and Healthy Thoughts," developed by Susan Kano, author of *Making Peace with Food*. By writing these thoughts down and repeating them regularly, you will get accustomed to affirming your individual strengths and congratulating yourself for your victories.

HAPPY AND HEALTHY THOUGHTS

1. I am a unique and precious human being, always doing the best I can, always growing in wisdom and love.
2. I don't need to prove myself to anyone—not even to myself—for I know that I am perfectly fine as I am.
3. I make my own decisions and assume responsibility for any mistakes. However, I refuse to feel shame or guilt about them. I do the best I can, and that is 100 percent good enough.

4. I am not my actions. I am the actor. My actions may be good or bad. That doesn't make me good or bad.
5. Whenever I am tempted to punish myself, I remember to be kind and gentle instead. I know that in order to be the best I can be, I need forgiveness and understanding.
6. I know that it is okay to need. I try to keep in touch with my needs so that I can respond to them.
7. I know that others cannot be expected to read my mind or to guess my needs. In fairness to them and to me, I ask for what I need.
8. I deserve to be appreciated. When others show their appreciation, I embrace it with open arms. I never try to deny or diminish my value.
9. I live one day at a time and do first things first.
10. I take great pride in what I do, in what I value, and in the way I live, for I truly believe in myself.
11. My mistakes and nonsuccess do not make a louse, a failure, or whatever. They only prove that I am imperfect, that is, human. It's wonderful to be human.
12. I love myself, absolutely and unconditionally, for that is what I truly need and deserve.

Although this list of affirmations is by no means absolute and complete, using it will help you to start thinking in more positive, constructive ways. However, I would strongly urge you to add your own *personal* affirmations to the list—the best things you can think or say about yourself. Be generous to yourself and give yourself proper credit for your strengths and achievements. These affirmations will give you added confidence and energy for change.

Carry your list of affirmations with you in your wallet or store it with your journal, diary, or appointment book, wherever it will be accessible, so you can refer to it daily. You may even want to post your affirmations on your refrigerator or the bathroom mirror, where you know they will catch your eye every day. Review and repeat your affirmations regularly and add to them whenever you can. Try not to feel foolish or self-conscious reading your affirmations aloud. Speaking and hearing these thoughts will lend them a special resonance and make them "more real" than if you simply read them on the printed page. Doing so will acknowledge and underscore your strengths.

The new power that you will begin to feel within yourself will soon spread outside yourself, too. In general, the better you feel about yourself, the better you will feel in your relationships to others. But if you need even more encouragement, you may also want to write an affirmation list about your relationships, especially the one with the alcoholic. Write down anything that honestly makes you feel good or hopeful about the alcoholic or the relationship between you. For example, you might write any of the following:

I appreciate that we are both pursuing our recovery.
I have very warm memories of our first meeting.
I still feel a great deal of love for _____ [the alcoholic], and _____ says that he [she] still loves me.
We both deserve to be happy, and I hope we can be happy together.

Try to personalize your relationship-affirmation list by including many more items of your own. Be as specific as you can. Reviewing this list will help keep you going whenever you run into some of the rough spots of relationship recovery—in the same way that your personal affirmation list will strengthen your individual recovery.

As the third item on the list of "Happy and Healthy Thoughts" suggests, guilt and shame often make positive affirmations impossible. Guilt is the feeling that you have done something "bad"; shame is the feeling that *you* are "bad." Although guilt feelings about specific actions are sometimes justified, codependents (and alcoholics) tend to feel excessive guilt and shame. These irrational and negative beliefs are often deeply rooted in what codependents see as "failures" and "worthlessness" of their past. If you feel burdened by guilt and shame, you will need to work to overcome these feelings. You will need to replace this faulty belief system with a kinder, gentler view of yourself. Only then will you be ready to acknowledge and accept your positive qualities.

Divide a piece of paper into two columns. In the left-hand column, list all the things about which you feel guilty or ashamed. In the right-hand column, write a positive affirmation that corrects each of these negative feelings about yourself. Through this exercise, you can begin to turn these undeserved put-downs into well-deserved praise. Although you will need to create a list of beliefs that are particular to you, here are a few suggestions to start you off:

SHAMEFUL BELIEF	TRUE STORY
1. I'm not important.	1. I'm very important.
2. I'm a bad person.	2. I was born innocent and am basically a good person—even with my flaws—which I am trying to correct.

SHAMEFUL BELIEF	TRUE STORY
3. I feel guilty because I failed to make the alcoholic stop drinking.	3. I never had any control over the alcoholic's drinking. No matter what I did or did not do, the alcoholic drank solely because she [he] is an alcoholic. I did the very best I could under the circumstances.
4. I'm worthless.	4. I deserve the very best life can offer.

When you have finished writing both lists, cross out every phrase in the first column. Then rewrite the second column, adding it to your personal list of affirmations.

Affirmations and acting as if can work hand in hand. Affirmations will help you see that you have a lot going for you, that you are worthwhile, and that you deserve to get better. Acting as if will motivate you to take the risks that will help you get better. By helping you see yourself in a new way, both will give you the strength and courage you need to continue to transform your life through recovery. Affirmations and acting as if will give you a powerful sense of personal accomplishment, suddenly making the impossible seem possible. This courageous and self-confident demonstration will transform your identity from a person who cannot to a person who can.

4

TAKING CARE OF YOURSELF

If you're like most codependents, you've probably been taking care of other people for most of your life. You've put others' needs ahead of yours and valued their feelings more than your own. But through your self-exploration as a Pioneer, you come to realize that you *do* matter. You discover that your needs and feelings are important and that you deserve to get what you want: your fair share of care, respect, and fun.

As a Pioneer, you will need to take the initiative if you really want to get what you want out of life. You can't just wait for the things you want to drop into your lap. If you want others to care for you, you will need to begin caring for yourself as much as you care for others. Similarly, if you want to win the respect of others, you need to begin by developing some self-respect. And you can start to have some fun simply by doing more frequently the things that give you pleasure. After years of self-denial, you deserve to get what you want. And though you can't *always* get what you want, you'll never get it if you don't try. So don't just wait for change to come to you; actively seek and promote change within and outside yourself.

PRIMARY CARE FOR THE CARETAKER

Like most recovering codependents, you probably spent a life-time taking care of other people's problems. But now, as a Pioneer, you need to start taking care of yourself and your own troubles. If you have learned to practice detachment, you know that you can't fix another person's problems. You need to let the alcoholic find his or her own answers and focus attention instead on finding solutions to your difficulties.

You may think you should have—and could have—taken care of all your troubles yesterday. After all, through years of practice, you probably became an expert problem solver. But tending to other people's dilemmas is often easier than trying to take care of your own. There's a lot less risk involved in telling someone else what to do than in attempting to do some-thing yourself. So try not to become too impatient to solve all your problems at once. Recognize that in taking care of your own problems, you are breaking new ground. Don't take on too much too soon or become overly self-critical when you "fail" to get all better overnight. You may need to work on developing less romantic expectations about what you can and cannot accomplish in recovery.

"I've gradually learned to lower some of my expectations of myself and my family, bringing them down to a more realistic level," confides David, whose mother and two brothers are all recovering from alcoholism or drug addiction. "I just find it so much easier and better when I don't put such high expectations on myself and everyone else. I guess it's mostly a matter of acceptance. I've started to accept who I am and who my family is. I no longer expect them to be any different from who they are.

"I guess it probably shouldn't be such a big surprise to me, but I'm learning that when I can avoid unrealistic expectations, when I don't ask myself to do too much or ask my family to give more than they can, I don't get discouraged or disap-pointed. When people come through for me the only way they know now, it's a pleasant surprise to me, rather than a huge disappointment. And if I achieve even more than I expected, I can congratulate myself."

If you constantly find yourself aiming too high, try to lower your sights a little. Certainly you should have aspirations and set goals for yourself. But putting extra pressure on yourself to do the impossible will only create unnecessary stress in your life. And this kind of tension truly makes it difficult for you to take care of yourself. When you find yourself faced with a personal challenge, give yourself permission to take as much time as you need to explore all your options. If you first review a variety of possible responses to the challenge, you can then make the wisest choice: the one that will best take care of you.

Many Pioneers find that repeating the Serenity Prayer (see Chapter 2) and then trying to live by it help relieve them of unwanted and unwarranted pressures. Using it helps slow them down, giving them time to consider their options. But it also allows them to separate the impossible—controlling something that's not in their power to control—from the achievable. The Serenity Prayer encourages Pioneers to take care of themselves by returning the focus of their efforts to themselves.

Does the Serenity Prayer work for you? Try to put it into practice by using this exercise. On a large, blank piece of paper, create three columns. Title the first column, "Things I Can Change"; the second column, "Things I Cannot Change"; and the third column, "Reasons." In the first column, list all the things you truly have the power to change: specific attitudes, behaviors, and ways you communicate. In the second column, write down the things you have no power to change: specific behaviors, thoughts, and feelings of other people. You probably have a rationale for why you've included each item in one column or the other. Write these reasons down in the third column. This list will remind you why you want to change some things and why you can't or don't need to make other changes. In preparing this list according to the Serenity Prayer, you will come to accept the impossible as impossible. This realization will allow you to focus on trying to achieve the possible: those things in the first column that you *can* change.

Betsy, a recovering codependent who regularly attends Al-Anon, tried this Serenity Prayer exercise after several months of individual therapy sessions with me. The first two lines of her list read as follows:

THINGS I CAN CHANGE	THINGS I CANNOT CHANGE	REASONS
1. My negative attitude		It will take away my excuse to behave unpleasantly toward myself and others.
2.	My husband's pessimism	I'm responsible only for my own attitude, not his.

By using this exercise, Betsy reinforced her commitment to live according to the Serenity Prayer. She provided herself with a concrete motivation to try to change the things she could. At the same time, she developed "the wisdom to know the difference" between the things she could and could not change. She gained a firm understanding of why she could not change things—such as her husband's mood—that were out of her control.

Are you willing to make the changes you have listed in the first column of the Serenity Prayer exercise? To be willing to change, you need to know that doing so is in your best interest. Ask yourself whether the thing you want to change is preventing you from taking good care of yourself. Betsy saw that her negative attitude was discouraging her from caring about what happened to herself or anyone else. She clearly realized that she needed—and wanted—to change that attitude.

Once you know that a specific change will do you some

good, prepare a plan of three or more steps and allow yourself a broad time frame for implementing each step. Betsy worked out the following plan to transform her persistent negativism:

1. Make a list of positive feelings I have about myself and others.
2. Recite this list to myself every day for two weeks.
3. Tell my best friend about these positive thoughts at the end of the two weeks.

Make sure to review your plan before putting it into action. Ask yourself, "Will this plan allow me to take better care of myself?" If, for example, Betsy had decided to change her negative attitude by suppressing all the anger she felt, that would have resulted in her taking *worse* care of herself. If you answer this question no, cross out the old plan and try to come up with a new one that will work for you. Make sure that you give yourself enough time to put the plan into action without putting too much pressure on yourself.

When Betsy reviewed her plan with me, she concluded, "Trying to develop more positive thinking and acknowledging the things I like about myself and other people will definitely be in my best interest. It will help increase my self-esteem and my acceptance of others." Betsy also decided that the time frame for her plan seemed realistic. But just in case, she added an optional fourth step to her plan:

4. If I am not convinced that my attitude has begun to change after the first three steps, I will repeat the steps for another two-week period.

With this small adjustment, Betsy set her plan into action, and it worked for her.

The Serenity Prayer exercise helped Betsy see that her primary responsibility was for herself. Like most Pioneers, Betsy had plenty of experience taking care of others, but little experience taking care of herself. Codependents and alcoholics seldom make any special effort to take care of themselves. Indeed, most recovering codependents and alcoholics need a little prompting to make even an ordinary effort to care for themselves. Are you taking care of yourself? Check this list to see whether you are making enough effort on your own behalf:

1. Do you eat regularly and have a balanced diet?
2. Do you get enough sleep and rest?
3. Have you established a balance between work and play in your life?
4. Do you regularly schedule leisure time and have fun?
5. Are you focusing on yourself?
6. Assess your responsibility: Are you doing too little, enough, or too much?
7. Are you forgetting about blame and letting go of old resentments?
8. Are you living in the present rather than in the past or the future?
9. Are you practicing the principles of the Twelve Steps in all your affairs?
10. Do you make your personal space as secure, safe, and serene as possible?
11. Can you ask for help whenever you need it?
12. Do you allow your program, your friends, and your sponsor to take care of you?

If you didn't reply to each item with a resounding yes, you need to pay more attention to these areas. Put some more effort into taking care of yourself in these ways. As you learn to take better care of yourself as a Pioneer, you will depend less and less on others to fill these voids. And this relaxation of demands will give your relationships the freedom to mature into Mutual Partnerships.

* * *

FACING FEELINGS

You've already spent some time trying to get in touch with your feelings. In the Eye-Opener stage, you worked to unearth some of the long-buried emotions from the past. Early in the Pioneer stage, you may have had to work past numbness—the inability to feel anything. Most alcoholics and codependents in recovery, however, find that they need to work on recognizing and expressing their emotions at *every* stage of recovery.

Facing up to your feelings is a big part of taking care of yourself and claiming the right and ability to get what you really want from life. You must recognize your needs and desires before you can begin to satisfy them or ask others to help satisfy them. And since our feelings play a key role in identifying our needs, you will have to own up to your emotions. If you continue to deny your feelings—as you probably did during the period of active alcoholism and codependency—you will never have a clear idea of what you want. But if you explore your feelings thoroughly and develop an informed notion of what you truly want and need, you will provide yourself with a clear direction for your personal and relationship recovery.

What do you still do to *avoid* feelings? How do you try to stifle or hide your feelings? Check the following list to see if you use any of these defenses against feelings:

- Eating too much
- Smoking
- Obsessive behavior involving alcohol or other drugs, gambling, sexuality, indebtedness, and so on
- Excessive physical activity
- Creating dramas in your life
- Relentless escapism into movies, television, books, and the like
- Overinvolvement with other people and *their* problems

If you engage in any of these activities as a way of burying your feelings, you will have to eliminate or curtail these behaviors. If you need help to change these behaviors, don't hesitate to seek it. A professional therapist can help you overcome many of these problems or put you in touch with people or groups that can help. Self-help support groups, such as Over-eaters Anonymous, Cocaine Anonymous, Sex Addicts Anonymous, and Debtors Anonymous, among many others, can help you address specific defense mechanisms that shut out feelings. Only after you have stopped clinging to these defenses will you truly be able to begin exploring your feelings.

Most Pioneers who have trouble facing their feelings need to deal with some unfinished business from the past. They may best begin by exploring old emotions that originally grew out of alcoholism and codependency but still linger in early recovery. Throughout the active period of the illness, suppression of emotions was the rule. But hidden emotions never really go away; they need to be released to dissipate. Unearthing these old feelings and trying to resolve them once and for all will pave the way for identifying and acknowledging your emotions today.

"When Hal was in the bars seven days a week, I thought of myself as the most miserable wife in the universe," remembers Caroline, a forty-five-year-old member of Al-Anon who identifies a lingering negative attitude as one of her major character defects. "I'd lie awake most nights, thinking what a jerk he was and what a witch I'd become. Of course, I never said anything about these feelings to Hal or to anyone else. I just kept everything to myself.

"Now Hal is sober and we've both been in our recovery programs for over a year. But I have to admit that much of my negativity about myself and my anger at him is still there. I didn't want to dump all this on Hal all at once—that wouldn't really be fair—but I knew I had to get it out of my system.

"Recently, with the help of my Al-Anon sponsor, I made a 'then' and 'now' list of negative feelings about myself and about him. Then I did the same with positive feelings. When I shared the lists with my Al-Anon friends, they pointed out that I had less negatives and more positives now than I did then. I was relieved to see that there was some change in the right direction, but not as much as I would have liked. I'm looking very hard at those 'negatives,' then and now, to see how I can reassess them or change them so they fit in the 'now positive' side of my ledger."

If you find yourself bogged down by the negativism of the past, you may want to try Caroline's exercise for yourself. Prepare your own lists and share them with your self-help sponsor or someone you trust. If you think you've already dealt with your past emotions in the Eye-Opener stage of recovery, you may want to concentrate solely on your "feelings now." In preparing your list of emotions, you may find it helpful to consult the list of "Unburied Feelings" included in Chapter 1.

If you have not yet done so, make a list of positive feelings to complement and balance the negative ones you've been carrying around for so long. Remember that facing your feelings means admitting your positive feelings as well as the negative ones. The following list may help you identify with some of those positive feelings. Like the list of "Unburied Feelings," this list of "Engouraging Feelings" is by no means all-inclusive. Therefore, you may want to add emotions of your own that were omitted from either list.

ENCOURAGING FEELINGS

adequacy	encouragement	pleasure
affection	enthusiasm	realism
balance	excitement	reasonableness
calmness	gladness	recognition
caring	gratitude	relaxation
cheerfulness	happiness	respect
confidence	harmony	restoration
connectedness	hopefulness	revitalization
contentment	joy	safety
curiosity	loved	satisfaction
eagerness	loving	self-assurance
elation	optimism	self-esteem
empowerment	peacefulness	self-worth

| serenity | sympathy | validation |
| spontaneity | understanding | wholeness |

Which of the feelings on this list or the list of "Unburied Feelings" do you feel today? You may want to go through the lists more than once, using different colored pens to check off the feelings you have regarding yourself and those you have toward your relationships. However you proceed, make sure you take the time to work through your feelings. Try following these guidelines:

1. *Identify your feelings.* Check off the ones that apply to you and check them again every few weeks to see how your feelings have changed. Before long, you won't need these formal lists to know how you feel.

2. *Allow yourself to experience your emotions fully, even if they are painful.* Don't forget to allow yourself to feel joy or happiness, too. You deserve positive feelings.

3. *Accept your feelings for what they are.* Understand that feelings are not "good" or "bad." They simply are. If you have difficulty accepting your emotions, you may find it helpful to identify, if you can, why you feel the way you do. Write sentences that begin "I feel loved because . . ." or "I feel depressed because . . ." or "I feel content because. . . ." Don't worry if you can't complete the sentence right away. But if you can pinpoint a cause, it may give you a clue to how to move beyond the feelings you want to change—and how to recapture at a later time the feelings you enjoy.

4. *Share your feelings with someone you love and trust.* In most cases, sharing anger, sadness, and negative emotions will help dissolve and diminish them. But paradoxically, sharing love, happiness, and other positive feelings has the opposite effect; it tends to help strengthen and expand them.

5. *Resolve your feelings.* Obviously, if you have tallied up many more negatives than positives, it means that either your self-esteem or your relationship needs more work. Using the sentence-completion exercise on page 97, try to think of ways that you could improve your feelings about yourself or your relationship. Try to accentuate the positive, acknowledging and affirming the uplifting feelings you have about yourself or your relationship. At the same time, continue to work through your negative feelings by sharing them with your group or therapist. Accept the feedback of the group or therapist, and if you receive advice that you consider worthwhile, take it.

SELECTIVELY SHARING YOUR FEELINGS

As a Pioneer, you need to concentrate on feeling your feelings and sharing them with others. But sharing feelings does *not* mean letting your feelings flood all over the place. If the alcoholic in your life is also in recovery, he or she is probably working on expressing emotions, too. In all likelihood, it will take a little time before either of you will know how to present your emotions in a nonaccusatory way. At the same time, you will both probably have to learn how to respond constructively to another person's honest expression of emotion, without hiding behind a wall of denial and defensiveness. These are skills that you will develop as Mutual Partners.

For now, though, each of you may need to practice "flood control" for a while. Controlling the flood of your feelings does *not* imply that you should dam them up again. You certainly need an outlet for your feelings, but you will probably find it most beneficial to avoid pouring them all out on the alcoholic. As you concentrate on improving your ability to express emotion, share your feelings with friends, sponsors, your therapist, or other members of your recovery program. Doing so will not only provide you with an emotional release, but will allow you to practice sharing your emotions honestly —a skill that will, in time, help improve your relationship with the recovering alcoholic.

"My husband finally told me he was sick of hearing about all my feelings all the time," admits Lucy, a criminal defense attorney. "He pointed out that most of the time we spent together I was talking about *my* life, *my* feelings, *my* recovery program, *my* day.

"For months, I've been complaining that Dick never tells me what he's feeling. Now that he's started, he's not saying exactly what I wanted him to say. But I think I needed to hear it anyway.

"Now I'm starting to understand where he is and where I am. Sure, it's great that I can finally feel my feelings and that I've developed my ability to share them, but Dick doesn't have to be my only dumping ground. He explained that his recovery is about his feelings, too. But we're at different places in our recovery, so he has a different kind of need. Right now, he needs time for quiet contemplation to figure out what he's actually feeling. By directing some of my feelings to other people. I can let him have the space he needs."

Increasing your ability to share feelings honestly and openly is a wonderful goal to set for yourself in recovery. But, as Lucy and Dick learned, you cannot simply "let it all hang out" all the time. If you want to share feelings constructively, you will need to make use of your internal "editor." Think before you speak: Consider whether you have chosen the right time, the right place, and the right person with whom to share. In perhaps four out of five situations, the sober alcoholic will be just the right person, but you need to have alternatives ready for that fifth case—when it would be better not to say anything or to share with someone else.

Do you recognize those times when it really would be better to keep your mouth closed rather than inform someone else of your feelings, opinions, or suggestions? Sharing feelings as a Pioneer requires this kind of sensitivity and selectivity. But constructive openness demands fairness as well. Do you allow for "fair sharing"? Do you listen to other people's thoughts and feelings, just as you expect them to listen to yours? Does your sharing end the conversation, or do you give others the opportunity to respond to the thoughts and feelings you've expressed? Remember that all you can do is provide the other person with the opportunity to speak. You cannot force the other person to share inner feelings or to speak honestly. For this reason, open communication works best when both people have made significant progress in their recovery. So concentrate on sharing your feelings with someone—preferably someone who will make an effort to understand and empathize.

RECOGNIZING YOUR STRENGTHS

Taking better care of yourself demands thinking better of yourself, for it is only when you believe that you *deserve* good things that good things will begin to come your way. I hope that your self-exploration has already begun to augment your feelings of self-worth. But if you are like most Pioneers, you will need to devote special effort to increasing your self-esteem. In looking at yourself, remember to acknowledge not only the areas you need to work on and your ability to improve these shortcomings, but your unique strengths, talents, and positive qualities. This recognition will breed self-confidence and affirm your inner strengths. Recognizing your wealth of positive traits will allow you to say, for perhaps the first time in your life, "I am who I am, I accept who I am, and I *like* who I am." Liking and accepting yourself pave the way for you to like, love, and accept others—and to have others like, love, and accept you.

"As long as I was a doormat, there were plenty of people willing to walk all over me," Pamela, a forty-year-old divorcée, now realizes. "But now that I think better of myself, I don't allow people to push me around or push my buttons anymore. As a result, I feel good and strong rather than weak and abused.

"Today, I see myself as an immovable object unless I *choose* to be moved. I've undergone a personal metamorphosis: from marshmallow to rock. The strength of my convictions about myself gives me a firm foundation in dealing with others. Learning to love myself has convinced me that I'm lovable to other people, too. And even though I'm not in a romantic relationship right now, I feel like I'm getting ready for one. I'm not worthless anymore. I've got a lot to offer, and I'm worth loving."

Pamela's growing awareness of her strengths has allowed her to transform herself through her recovery. She has begun to move away from her preoccupation with labeling her liabilities and has moved toward acknowledging her real abilities. She now knows that she had a number of good qualities all along, traits that went unrecognized for far too long. But just as important, she also realizes her own power to improve on her faults, to change and transform herself. This new self-respect and empowerment confirm that Pamela has accomplished one of the primary goals of the Pioneer stage: to build a solid sense of herself and her strengths. Instead of coming into every relationship as an inferior, she is now ready to enter new relationships on an equal level. She is prepared to be a Mutual Partner.

If you have difficulty acknowledging your strengths, you may find it helpful to start by accepting the compliments of others. You may have put yourself down for so long that you find it difficult to allow others to boost you. If on some deep level you still feel essentially worthless, you will probably have a tendency to reject any favorable comments. You may find yourself responding to compliments with minimizing remarks, objections that usually begin with the word "But."

In rejecting other people's compliments, you reveal your lack of trust—in them as well as in yourself. If you don't believe yourself worthy of compliments, you may doubt other people's motivations in saying something positive about you. If you lived with an especially manipulative alcoholic (or codependent), your history may even justify a little suspicion regarding other people's good intentions. But if you instinctively react to every compliment by wondering, "What's in it for them?" or

"What are they trying to get from me?" then you no longer have the ability to trust the good judgment of others.

As a Pioneer, you need to work on trying to trust the judgment of others even when you're not sure you can. When someone compliments you, try to delight in this praise, rather than discount it. You can learn to accept compliments gracefully by gradually changing your responses. For example:

- When someone pays you a compliment, simply try to say, "Thank you." Stop yourself from reacting with your "But. . . ."
- Start by thinking that the favorable opinion expressed by that other person *may* be right. This "trusting as if" is a variation on the principle "acting as if."
- Try to trust the *person* as well as the compliment. Trust "as if" the person who has validated you is not "wrong," "stupid," "misinformed," or "manipulative." Who knows? Maybe he or she is right and doesn't demand anything in return for the compliment.

Increasing your ability to accept compliments can help begin to augment your sense of self-worth. But ultimately, self-esteem needs to come from within you. You cannot depend exclusively on others to provide you with a sense of approval, although they *can* offer you a lot of support. You need to discover and acknowledge your own strengths, developing a positive vision of yourself that will sustain you in your efforts to recover and grow.

If you still feel unsure of your many assets, strengths, and accomplishments, you may find it beneficial to construct a personal honor roll. The honor roll allows you the long-overdue opportunity to salute yourself for your talents and achievements. Try to think of all the specific attributes for which you deserve credit. List them on a piece of paper, and for each quality, cite as least three instances—past or current—in which you demonstrated that trait to a high degree. Recipients of congressional or presidential medals of honor accept citations that salute their courage and valor. Why shouldn't you get the same recognition?

By this point in your recovery, you can probably identify most of your own strengths. For some additional suggestions, consult the following list:

perseverance	leadership
warmth	intelligence
honesty	flexibility
patience	perceptiveness
reliability	caring
self-starting ability	trouble-shooting skills
resilience	diligence
responsibility	crisis-management expertise
competence	determination
desire to improve	generosity
courage	love
loyalty	cooperativeness
trustworthiness	good-natured disposition
energy	humor

Almost all the Pioneers I've met through my practice have demonstrated most of these qualities. They deserve honor and recognition—at the very least, from themselves—for each of them.

Building your self-esteem will set in motion a cycle that will lead to better and stronger relationships. By gaining the ability to replace self-reproach with self-respect, you will concentrate more on your abilities than on your liabilities. Recognizing your worth and strength will help you focus on recent achievements and current goals, rather than on the painful hurts and losses of the past. The hopelessness of the past will fade, supplanted by a new hope—one bred from confidence in your power and in the overall benevolence of other people and a Higher Power. And this new hope will give you the strength you need to overcome present difficulties and meet future challenges. With this new confidence in the present and hope for the future, you will find it easier to live in the now, enjoying yourself and your loved ones.

LETTING YOURSELF HAVE FUN

If you're like most codependents or alcoholics in the Pioneer stage of recovery, enjoying yourself may be an entirely new experience for you. When the disease of alcoholism is in full swing, there are few real swingers. Most active alcoholics try desperately to "have a good time," but they usually succeed only in deluding themselves: They start thinking that drinking is the only way they can have fun. Even this delusion disintegrates as the disease takes greater and greater control of alcoholics' lives. Indeed, most recovering alcoholics describe their final drinking days as terrible times when they could neither get drunk nor get sober. Far from having fun, they were in a perpetual state of despair. Codependents, like the alcoholics who dominate their lives, have usually reached the end of their emotional ropes by the time they finally get treatment for themselves. Most codependents stay so busy trying to take care of everyone and everything that they don't have any energy left for fun. By the time the "party" is over, everyone trying to clean up the mess it has left agrees: It wasn't any fun at all.

With sobriety, however, comes the end of despair and the beginning of hope for a new life. When you were an Eye-Opener, you may never have dared contemplate the possibility of enjoying yourself. The deadly serious business of stopping your codependent or alcoholic behavior may have left you with little energy for recreation. But by now, in the Pioneer stage, you can begin to look upon your recovery as an opportunity to bring some enjoyment into your life. As you continue to heighten your sense of self-esteem, remind yourself that as a worthwhile individual, you deserve both fun and joy.

"I haven't been dancing since high school," reminisces Winnie, a forty-seven-year-old Pioneer. "I never really learned ballroom dancing, and I never enjoyed it anyway. And when all the new rock and roll music came into vogue, I was much too embarrassed to get out on a dance floor and do the twist, or do the monkey, or do whatever people were doing in the sixties.

"But then a couple of months ago, a few of my Al-Anon friends dragged me to a neighborhood church where they have old-fashioned country square dancing. It's so much fun! I just can't believe I'm enjoying it so much. I had always stayed home on Saturday nights because I considered them 'date nights,' and I never had any dates. But people don't go to these dances with 'dates.' They just go to have a good time. And now, so do I."

Don't feel embarrassed about having a little fun. You deserve it. If you begin to feel embarrassed, try laughing instead. Since most embarrassment springs from our tendency to take ourselves too seriously, a good sense of humor can work wonders. You may not have been able to appreciate the humor of certain situations in you life before. Things may have seemed far too dire to laugh at them. But as the laughter often heard in AA and Al-Anon meetings proves, recovery permits both alcoholics and codependents to recapture their sense of humor.

As you develop a healthier perspective about yourself and others, you will also regain or develop a sense of humor. You will realize that the world won't come to an end just because you do something silly, foolish, or embarrassing. So try not to take yourself so seriously. If you take some chances and pursue the things you have fun doing, you will experience firsthand the sheer exhilaration that comes with joy. Lightening up your attitude and incorporating fun things into your lifestyle may initially seem intimidating. But as Winnie discovered, despite her fear, it's well worth exploring.

What do you enjoy doing? Look into the activities in your community and see whether you can find something enjoyable or even exciting to do that you've never done before or something that you enjoyed doing long ago. Perhaps you'd like to try camping out in a nearby state park. Or maybe you'd like to go to a ball game, rather than just watch it on television. Better still, you could play some ball or perhaps a couple of sets of tennis at the local YMCA. You may prefer visiting one of the art or cultural museums or exhibitions in your area. Whether you prefer throwing Frisbees or throwing pots, hooking fish or hooking rugs, spending a night in a tent or a night at the opera, you can probably find a place to have some fun in your area.

Don't wait for others to take the initiative and bring fun to you. Go after it yourself. You can have a good time with friends, groups, or on your own. Over time, as both you and the alcoholic continue to pursue your individual recoveries, you will discover how to have fun together—again or for the first time. You will learn how to plan fun things to do as a couple or a family and share in each other's joy. But you don't need to put your own fun on hold while you wait for someone else.

"My boyfriend Al has been sober for over a year, but he never initiates anything for us to do together," Peg complains. "It's up to me to make all the social plans, and I get really frustrated with that. I don't want to be stuck in that responsible and controlling position anymore.

"Recently we kept talking about going to see this movie. As usual, I kept waiting for him to suggest a time and a date, but he never got around to it. One day, a friend asked me to go see the movie with her, so I did. Al was really upset. He couldn't understand how I could go without him. I reminded him that he had promised over and over again to take me to see the film, but had never followed through. I wanted to see it, so I went. I'm still not sure Al understands, but it was a big step for me. Al couldn't take care of us, so I took care of me."

By seizing some of the fun that's all around you, you can make your life more satisfying and worthwhile, no matter what anyone else chooses to do. So as part of your recovery, remember to have fun while exploring yourself, too. Although the self-discovery that comes through the work of the Pioneer stage will sometimes cause you pain or discomfort, it should also bring you a great deal of joy and delight. If you learn to combine the equally important components of work and play in your personal recovery, you will gradually gain the ability to transfer this balance to all other areas of your life as well. You will know how to have fun whether you're working on yourself, trying to improve a relationship, handling a challenge on the job, or enjoying one of your leisure-time activities. This newfound ability to have fun can give birth to a revitalized spirit, a renewed passion for life and all its wonders.

"Looking at my three-year-old daughter made me realize that the same wonderful natural enthusiasm she has, that absolute wonder and delight she gets about things, is something both my sister and I have managed to retain, too," says Evelyn, still exulting in the revelation. "Initially, we got it from our mother, and I feel a lot of gratitude for that quality today. Even though my mother was an active alcoholic until just two years ago and she certainly has her share of faults and inadequacies, I had forgotten about that wildly enthusiastic view of life that she always had, even at the height of her disease. I give myself a big plus for recapturing that enthusiasm in my own life and then passing it along to my daughter. It's really great to love life again."

5

AVOIDING OBSTACLES
TO RECOVERY

The road to recovery is not necessarily smooth every step of the way. When you were an Eye-Opener, the persistence of denial may have occasionally blotted out your new awareness of the impact of alcoholism and codependency. Long after your eyes first opened to the nature of these illnesses, you may have suffered from extended periods of recurrent denial, temporarily blocking your growth and stalling your recovery. Ultimately, however, you overcame your denial, began to practice detachment and establish appropriate boundaries, and became a Pioneer on a journey of self-discovery.

As a Pioneer, you have undoubtedly made great strides in your recovery. You know yourself much better and have regained a *real* sense of control over your life. Even as a Pioneer, though, you may run into some roadblocks that temporarily stall your recovery, preventing you from seeing yourself clearly. No matter how much you want to change and how much work you put into it, you may occasionally feel as if you are standing still or slipping backward. You may revert to old patterns of thinking or behavior that impede your personal growth and your efforts to improve your relationships. Indeed, you may get so frustrated that you even think of ending the journey altogether. It may seem like more work than you bargained for.

If you sometimes feel this way, try not to give in to such despair. The new self-awareness that has arisen through your inner exploration as a Pioneer demands constant vigilance. By definition, this awareness must include an alertness to the personal danger zones within you that threaten to sabotage your recovery.

This chapter will alert you to some of the most common dangers that stand in the way of Pioneering self-exploration: entertaining second thoughts about the need for change, recognizing and dealing with stressful situations or circumstances, blaming others, and blaming yourself. It may ease some of your frustration if you know that others have overcome these same obstacles. If and when you encounter these difficulties, take the time you need to figure out the best way to offset these threats to your new sense of balance, your emotional well-being, and your improving relationships. Calm, caution, and confidence will carry you through these danger zones. The better you know yourself, the easier it will become to recognize these difficulties and take the appropriate steps to avoid slipping backward in recovery.

HOW MUCH DO YOU WANT TO CHANGE?

Of all the obstacles to personal growth, the biggest by far is your reluctance to change. No matter how much people may say they want to change, most of them initially try to avoid taking the steps that will bring change about. In the Pioneer stage of recovery, you need to examine your struggle to avoid change. Most Pioneers tend to welcome some changes while delaying or rebelling against certain others. You may, for example, warmly embrace the opportunity to begin talking about your feelings. The immediate sense of relief you feel may even reinforce your willingness to make this change part of your day-to-day life. But at the same time, you may feel reluctant to let go of your resentments—or perhaps your arrogance or your compulsion to manage things.

A wide variety of emotions and attitudes can impede your progress in the growth process by "justifying" your resistance to change. You may not want to give up managing, for instance, because you think that "things will fall apart if I don't take care of everything." Or you may recognize your arrogance as a flaw, but still not want to give it up because you believe "It helps me get ahead" or "It's an essential part of my personality." If you feel this way about some of your flaws, try to recognize rationalization for what it is: an attempt to excuse yourself from giving up your faults. You've grown accustomed to your flaws and perhaps even love some of them. And this makes it awfully hard to let them go.

"The Sixth and Seventh Steps say that I need to be willing to give up my character defects and then ask God to remove them. The one I have the most trouble with is my arrogance," admits Patrick, a trial lawyer. "I've come to be viewed a certain way in my profession and I've been successful at it. While some people may not like my haughtiness, they can see that my style gets results in the courtroom.

"For a long time, I felt people would think I was a 'wimp' if I stopped strutting my stuff the way I usually do. And I used that feeling, and my track record in the courtroom, to convince myself that I didn't really need to work on it. But the truth of the matter is that by becoming less arrogant, I'm getting more positive reactions than I ever expected. That arrogance was just false confidence anyway. It covered up my fear. I thought I was fooling people, but I guess I wasn't. The real me isn't nearly as confident as I come off. And people seem to like me when I'm more myself.

"I was probably even more arrogant at home than in the courtroom. I thought everything had to be done my way because my way was the only way. But now we sit down as a family and actually discuss problems and everyone has input.

Helen has helped a lot. She just doesn't let me get away with that kind of attitude anymore. She says, 'Excuse me, your ego is showing.' That's her way of letting me know I am being arrogant again."

As Patrick did, you may fear that you'll become a "person without a personality" if you give up your most discernible flaws. You may begin to wonder, "Why should I be so willing and ready to have the defects I have identified removed from my character? After all, that's part of who I am." Indeed, your faults do linger as part of who you are now. But you could have said the same about the illnesses of codependency and alcoholism. They are certainly part of who you are, too. Yet they have become part of your *past,* because you chose to leave them behind.

You may sometimes forget what things were like in the past, when you were stuck in an alcoholic/codependent relationship. You may not recall how unhappy you were when alcoholism ruled every aspect of your environment. And you may not remember how all your flaws contributed to your misery. But as philosopher and poet George Santayana wrote almost a century ago, "Those who cannot remember the past are condemned to repeat it." If you forget your codependent tendency to become overinvolved in other people's problems, for example, you may let down your guard and unintentionally cross the personal boundary line you had previously set for yourself. Or you may hold on to your arrogance, forgetting that for years this trait made it impossible for you to ask for the help you needed.

Whenever you feel overly attached to one of your faults, try to "keep your memories green." Going to Al-Anon or AA meetings can help remind you how things were way back when. In this context, ask yourself what part your faults played in your ongoing codependency or alcoholism —and, hence, in your prolonged misery. The Pioneer stage of recovery demands that you begin to make these sorts of connections. This thorough and purposeful self-examination will not only help you see yourself more clearly, it will give you extra motivation for self-improvement. If you see how these faults added to your unhappiness, you will see the advantage of giving them up.

No matter how consciously determined you are to give up your character defects, however, you may find yourself unconsciously reverting to old ways when things in your life get too stressful. You may embrace change in times of calm, but for most Pioneers, resistance to change tends to increase whenever anything threatens that serenity. Old attitudes and behavior, the residue of unconscious resistance, rush in on the heels of turbulence. The strain of fatigue, work or family pressures, emergencies or temporary crises, or other stressful situations can sometimes resuscitate outmoded patterns.

Although you cannot always avoid external stresses—a new boss, for example, or a death in the family—you can take measures to reduce the amount of stress you create internally. What do you do that increases the pressures of your everyday life? Perhaps you allow resentments against the alcoholic to build up inside you. Or maybe you find yourself getting angry all the time for "no reason." You know better than anyone what sorts of feelings and behaviors tend to upset your equilibrium. Each of these things, by increasing the pressure in your life, can set back your personal and relationship recovery. You will need to find pressure valves—self-help groups or a therapist perhaps—that will permit you to let off some of this pressure. You may find it helpful to make a list of your personal *toxins:* the things, both internal and external, that can be poisonous to your personal and relationship growth. What attitudes, emotions, and circumstances—*or even people*—make you feel off balance and get you off track of recovery? What feelings or situations bring out your resentments and your unconscious resistance to change? You cannot afford to let these toxins sidetrack you from getting better. To further your personal recovery, you may need to put these toxins aside for a while. Until you can build up your immunity (your self-esteem and inner strength), try to avoid these toxins whenever you can.

"When I am exhausted or not up to par physically, my head

does strange things," explains Joanna, a forty-five-year-old office manager. "I start telling myself that nobody really cares for me, and I can get right back into my old attitude of self-pity. I want to get into bed, pull the covers over my head, and lie there being miserable. I tell myself that with Bill at his AA meetings seven nights a week, I'm just as alone as ever. What's the difference? It's just like he was out drinking again. I feel abandoned, and then I use his absence to justify my sorry, neglected state.

"But I can see that's very dangerous thinking. I mean, I know there's a big difference between what things are like now and what they were like then. Ignoring that difference and pitying myself only leads to my isolation, and that's always been a big part of my disease. Today I have a choice. I can feel sorry for myself or do something different. It isn't always easy to jump out of bed and call an Al-Anon friend or get myself to a meeting. But I know that's what I have to do.

"I made up my own acronym to help me in those times. I say to myself, 'Don't be DAFT.' For me, DAFT means Depressed, Angry, Frustrated, or Tired. Those are the things I really have to watch out for, the things that get me into trouble. Now I can identify the things that bring out my resentments and try to ward them off. That way, I won't fall back into that negative, passive, hopeless position I remember so well."

Can you identify with any of the danger signs pinpointed by Joanna's DAFT acronym? Joanna modeled her warning sign after a slogan commonly used in Al-Anon and other Twelve-Step programs: "HALT—Don't get too Hungry, Angry, Lonely, or Tired." You may use DAFT or HALT as a reminder of things you should guard against. Or, as you continue to explore yourself, make up your own acronym. From your list of toxins, select a few that are particularly virulent, the circumstances that most often threaten your peace of mind. Then play with the initials of these personal danger signs a little until you come up with a warning of your own. Some of my patients have come up with the following suggestions:

Don't be a BLOB: Blaming, Lonely, Off centered, or Blue.
Avoid coming in LAST: Lonely, Angry, Self-centered, or Tense.
Don't feel RAW: Resentful, Anxious, or Worthless.
Don't get LOST: Lonely, Obsessed, Sad, or Tired.

Although these kinds of acronyms spell out your best intentions to avoid these danger signs, you can't always prevent yourself from having these feelings. If you occasionally slip, don't condemn yourself as a failure. Just reach out for some help and get back on track as quickly as you can. The most important thing is to remain willing and ready to change, to try to build character and work toward improvement without feeling you have to be perfect. All of us are flawed beings, yet recovery helps us work on overcoming our faults.

Fundamentally, like all Pioneers, you know that it's vital to your recovery to keep trying to improve yourself. You may alternately approach and avoid change, but ultimately you recognize that you need to maintain your movement toward moral, spiritual, emotional, and intellectual growth. The "searching and fearless moral inventory" that began with the Fourth Step will continue throughout your life. You will constantly discover new flaws in yourself. Yet each new discovery will offer you a fresh challenge and opportunity to grow: by deciding if, when, and how you can give up your defect. As a Pioneer, you surely recognize that like all human beings, you will never achieve perfection. But you can't let that realization stop you from trying to improve yourself, to become the best *you* that you can be.

BLAMING OTHERS AND BLAMING OURSELVES

One of the most powerful factors that encourages us to avoid change is the human tendency to blame others for our own difficulties. In relationships between alcoholics and codependents, the drinkers most often receive the brunt of this blame. While actively pursuing their addictions, alcoholics set themselves up as targets for all a family's troubles. Most of those who are close to an alcoholic tend to think that the other person's drinking has led to all their problems. Codependents find it easy to condemn the alcoholic for their neglected friendships, personal failures, and a host of unresolved problems. Any uncomfortable feelings—from relentless anger, annoyance, and outrage to devastating sadness and despair—can be easily blamed on the active alcoholic. But once the alcoholic has sobered up or you have chosen to shift your focus to your problems, rather than those of the alcoholic, you may find it harder to blame her or him—or even the disease of alcoholism —for all your difficulties.

Blame is one of the most difficult issues you'll need to confront while on the road to recovery. As you explore yourself in the Pioneer stage of recovery, you may still find that you are tempted to blame certain faults or character flaws on others— especially the alcoholic. Since people who are stuck in blame refuse to change their attitudes or behavior unless someone else changes first, their personal recovery is blocked. Blame demands that others measure up to your standards. But as long as you're standing still—waiting for others to meet your expectations before you'll put any effort into changing one of your faults—you can't move ahead in your own recovery. Censuring someone else for your troubles falsely strips you of any ability—or responsibility—to change. In blaming others, you put all power over your life into another person's hands— just as you did when you were in the grip of codependency.

"My husband Tony got sober six months ago. I know it's a big mistake for me to worry about if and when he is going to start to change—or at least change the way I want him to change," stresses Teresa, a librarian in her thirties. "But at times, I make that mistake anyway. I blame him for not changing fast enough to suit my liking.

"I start to obsess about how wonderful *my* life would be if *he* got a hard-nosed sponsor and worked the Steps, if *he* were interested in my recovery program the same way I'm interested in his, if *he* stopped criticizing me, if *he* were more affectionate, if *he* didn't have such big mood swings, if *he* could share more of his feelings with me, if *he* appreciated me. . . . I could go on forever with all these 'ifs.' My sponsor keeps telling me that unless it has a direct impact on me, what he says, thinks, or does is none of my business now. My primary business is my recovery. I need to take the responsibility to change whether or not he changes."

Blaming others for not acting the way you would like them to behave, as Teresa discovered, involves a lot of useless "if only" thinking. Blame rests on the false assumption that "If only he hadn't done this" or "If only she wouldn't do that," then you would have had a perfect life and a perfect relationship. But think back to one of the first times you had a thought like this: "If only the alcoholic would stop drinking, everything would be fine." Now that the alcoholic in your life has stopped drinking, you know that sobriety has not made all your problems miraculously disappear. Resolving your problems together will take work by both of you, not just wishful thinking.

Certainly life would be more peaceful "if only" everyone would behave the way we wanted him or her to behave (although it would also be terribly boring). Since other people are not under our control, however, wishing and blaming will never make someone else change. They simply allow the blamer and wisher to accumulate a storehouse of resentments. When Teresa was in a blaming mode, for example, every time her husband's behavior didn't conform to her expectations, she added another resentment to her collection. She had stopped looking at what she could do to improve the situation, focusing instead on what her husband should do.

When you denounce others in this way, you bring your personal growth and the improvement of your relationships to a dead stop. In blaming another person—or another person's behavior—for your own problems, you focus all your energy and attention on someone else's past actions, rather than on your present ones. Ultimately, this behavior can only serve as an excuse to avoid change yourself. Because they hold on to the past and refuse to let it go, blamers become stagnated in their recovery.

"My kid brother Joel was the black sheep of our family," explains Dennis, a chemical engineer who blamed his personal problems on his brother for years. "And since I was the hero, I felt it was my job to save him. I signed up very willingly. It was much easier for me to concentrate on keeping him out of jail and getting him into hospitals than on dealing with my own life. I spent years looking out for him just so I wouldn't have to look at myself.

"He gave me the perfect excuse for never having a serious romance. Whenever I'd start to get close to a woman, I'd end up going off on another rescue mission. I'd think nothing of canceling my plans because I *had to* take care of my 'poor brother.' And when things fell apart—and they always did—I blamed him for my failed romances.

"Joel's sober now; he's been doing great for a year and a half. But now that he doesn't need me to rescue him, I can't avoid dealing with my fear of intimacy anymore. I see how much I blamed him to cover up my fears. The fact was, I was terrified of close relationships. I now realize that I'm alone because the idea of being with anyone else scares me to death. Joel didn't stifle my romances; I did. So I can't blame him anymore."

For most of his adult life, Dennis had used his brother as an excuse to avoid exploring the reasons he had never formed any sort of meaningful relationship. To move toward outside relationships, he needed to stop blaming Joel's "helplessness" and start to examine and help himself. Unfortunately, Dennis did not become ready, willing, or able to begin that introspection until after Joel became sober. Pioneers who are stuck in their blame point an accusing finger at someone else and scold, "You're wrong, you change." But when Joel *did* change, Dennis had nowhere else to look but at himself. So whenever you feel tempted to blame someone else for your difficulties, remember that the same hand that can point one finger outward in reproach has three fingers that can point inward. If you find yourself constantly blaming others for your troubles, you're not taking responsibility for your own.

When both you and the alcoholic in your life became actively engaged in recovery programs, you come to realize that it takes (at least) two to tangle. Indeed, your recovery depends on this realization. Your healing as a Pioneer demands that you explore *your* participation in the problems of your relationship or your family. Have you taken a complete and thorough personal inventory yet? Who do you blame for your past and present troubles? In most addictive relationships, everyone around the alcoholic gets involved in keeping the illness going. What did you find when you looked at your involvement in this family disease? What role did you play? Did you consciously or unconsciously participate in the cover-up that helped perpetuate the illness, as Dennis did "for" his brother?

In looking at yourself and your relationships in this way, try not to judge yourself too harshly. Self-blame can be even more destructive to personal recovery than can blaming others. Self-blame most often springs from the sense of hyperresponsibility that many codependents feel. You may admonish yourself for "not doing enough" to stop the alcoholic from drinking. Or you may blame yourself for "causing" all the misfortunes of everyone around you. But just as blaming others can exempt you from the responsibility to change on your own, self-blame relieves others of accountability for their actions. By ignoring the fact that you cannot change someone else, you discourage, through self-blame, others from taking responsibility for themselves.

"My codependency is most obvious in the way I assume responsibility for things that aren't my responsibility in my family," acknowledges Kit, a computer programmer who is trying to stop blaming herself for the alcoholism of other members of her family. "I know now that I can't do or not do anything that will make my sister keep drinking or get sober. What I do or don't do is not going to determine whether my husband, who's been sober for six months now, picks up a drink again. For years, I've wanted to help my father find his way to AA. Today I know that I may be able to tell him how his disease affects me, but I can't make him get into treatment. Unless he's ready to make that move, he won't do it—no matter what I do.

"So I'm starting to realize that I can't blame myself for what my family does or doesn't do. I mean, it's not easy to stop blaming myself after so many years of practice, but I'm trying. I'm starting to accept the fact that all I really have responsibility for is my own recovery. What I do or don't do for myself is entirely up to me. My choices and my actions are what make me who I am. For that, and only for that, I am responsible."

Many recovering Pioneers stop themselves in their tracks by obsessing over the things they "could have done," "should have done," or "didn't do." They blame themselves unmercifully for all the wrong things they have done or the right things they haven't done in their lives. Like blaming others, though, this kind of thinking leaves Pioneers stuck in the past, instead of moving forward. By focusing on the imaginary possibilities of the past, people who are mired in self-blame ignore the potential to make amends in the present. Many Pioneers use the Eighth and Ninth Steps of AA to help them move forward. In applying the Eighth Step, you will begin to understand that although you always tried to do the best you could, you made mistakes in the past that hurt others as well as yourself. The Ninth Step then encourages you to make amends unless those attempts to repair the damage would further harm others. This step means not just saying that you are sorry, but taking actions that *show* that you feel sorry and that try to heal any injuries you may have inflicted. Making reparations wherever you can will allow you to put the past behind you once and for all and resume your forward progress in recovery.

Giving up both blame and self-blame has helped Kit and Dennis find new acceptance and honesty in their lives. By starting to distinguish between their responsibilities and those of others, they both have begun to establish a sense of balance in their lives. Since Kit no longer heaps excessive blame on herself, she has relinquished the responsibility to try to change others. Instead, she is now trying to accept others the way they are. And since Dennis no longer heaps excessive blame on others—especially his brother—for his difficulties, he has started to look at himself and accept himself the way he is: as an imperfect being who is sincerely and diligently trying to overcome his fears and shortcomings and to change for the better. This more realistic assessment and acceptance of themselves and others has formed the basis for a new honesty in Kit's and Dennis's lives. And this new honesty will allow and encourage greater intimacy in their personal relationships today and tomorrow.

OVERCOMING OBSTACLES: THE END OF ISOLATION

The obstacles to recovery discussed in this chapter all get in the way not only of personal growth, but of the development of close relationships. By now, you recognize that the rules that govern codependent behavior prevent intimacy—both within and outside the alcoholic relationship. Active alcoholics and codependents cannot get truly close to each other because their illnesses make it impossible to deal with each other honestly and openly as equals. At the same time, they tend to close everyone else out of their lives to protect the "secret" of alcoholism. Codependents and alcoholics alike end up feeling isolated and alone. In recovery, any second thoughts or stress that Pioneers allow to inhibit or block change keep them tied to the codependent alienation of the past.

Like most recovering codependents (and alcoholics), your greatest flaws probably tend to isolate you from others. Self-pity, for instance, can cause you to withdraw from others. Arrogance can prevent you from asking others for the help you need. Each harbored resentment can further distance you from another person. Trying to manage other people's lives places you above them, making an intimate relationship between equals impossible. Look at your own faults, the ones you listed in compiling your personal inventory in accordance with the Fourth Step of AA and Al-Anon. How do they continue to contribute to your isolation and loneliness? Do any of them prevent you from dealing with others as equals—that is, by positioning yourself above or below other people in your esteem? If your flaws make equality impossible in your relationships or add to your loneliness in any way, then why should you hold on to them any longer?

Blaming others and self-blame also further isolation and prevent Pioneers from moving toward Mutual Partnerships. Both attitudes tend to exalt one person and debase the other in a relationship, instead of allowing for interaction between equals. In blaming others or yourself, you place all power and responsibility into one person's hands—and the person in power *always* does the wrong thing. For this reason, both types of blame are one-way dead-end streets. Since blaming closes the door to honest communication, both negotiation and compromise become impossible.

Since blaming, self-blame, and so many codependent character defects increase loneliness, any refusal to give up these flaws prevents Pioneers from moving out of their isolation. In giving up these faults and embracing personal recovery as a Pioneer, however, you will inevitably draw closer to others. The new honesty and self-acceptance that come from recognizing and trying to improve your faults will encourage you to extend that same honesty and acceptance to others, thawing your sense of isolation. And the restored sense of balance between yourself and others, an equilibrium bolstered by giving up blame and self-blame, will allow you to deal with others on an equal footing. By overcoming these obstacles, you will declare an end to the isolation of the past. And the inevitable improvement of your relationships will at last permit you to move into a Mutual Partnership.

The Mutual-Partner Stage

6

STILL TOGETHER—BUT CAN WE RECOVER TOGETHER?

Congratulations! You've come a long way on your road to recovery! Your dedication to your recovery and your commitment to others is admirable. As an Eye-Opener, you discovered new truths about the family illnesses of addiction. You bravely confronted the alcoholism of someone you loved, as well as your own codependency. And you established your own program of recovery. During the Pioneer stage, you undertook a challenging journey of self-exploration. You investigated your needs, wants, and desires and ultimately discovered your inner self. In pursuing your own, newly recognized goals, you learned to be cautious and avoid danger, yet still move consistently and courageously forward on your path to recovery.

Through your work with those involved in your immediate recovery program—members of Al-Anon, your therapist, and other helpers—you have gained a new perspective on intimacy, as well as a more accurate understanding of yourself and your recovery. You not only know who you are and what you want from your life in recovery, but you can see yourself in relation to others. You have practiced more open and honest interaction with those in your recovery program and you have no doubt formed real, lasting, and substantial relationships with many of them. Now, though, you need to broaden your perspective to look more closely at who you are and how you behave in your most important personal relationships, not only those within your recovery program, but those within your home—with the alcoholic, if he or she is still a part of your life, and other members of your family. You are ready to form Mutual Partnerships in *all* your important relationships with others.

In the Mutual-Partner stage of recovery, you will learn to apply the principles of personal recovery—drawn from your self-help group or groups, your therapist, and this book—to your most intimate relationships. By now, since you have probably grown much more comfortable with working your personal recovery program, you also probably feel more comfortable in your daily life outside "the rooms"—the place where your self-help group meets. Indeed, the Twelfth Step of AA encourages us to take recovery beyond the confines of these rooms and "to practice these principles in all our affairs." In working toward Mutual Partnership, you will aim toward this goal by continuously integrating the principles of individual recovery into the growth and development of your personal relationships.

You can strive toward Mutual Partnership in any relationship: as a heterosexual couple, a homosexual couple, close friends, siblings, parents and adult children, or even an extended family. In the coming chapters, I will focus primarily on relationships involving romantic love. However, with the obvious exception of Chapter 10, which concentrates solely on improving sexual intimacy, you can apply all the principles and suggestions offered to couples to any of your relationships —with siblings, parents, adult children, and friends, as well as with spouses or lovers. Any adults who are tied by a strong emotional bond and are recovering from addiction or codependency or both can improve their relationships through the work of the Mutual-Partner stage of recovery. Regardless of the specific nature of the relationship, the principles involved in building strong, mutually fulfilling relationships remain the same.

COMMITMENT, COMMON GOALS, AND COMMUNICATION

Commitment, common goals, and communication—the three Cs of Mutual Partnership—are the cornerstones of any relationship in recovery. Before you begin the serious work of relationship recovery, you may find it helpful to assess how well your relationship works right now. Do you and the alcoholic have a strong working alliance, a solid commitment to each other and to the partnership? Do you both put the good of the relationship before your own or your partner's self-interest? Do you both know when to focus on yourselves and when to focus on your partner or on the partnership? Do you each feel confident that you are working *together* to improve your partnership? Do you share common goals and plan together to come up with approaches to achieving these goals? Do you both give to the relationship and get something out of it? In relating to and communicating with your partner, do you offer the same attention, honesty, openness, love, and respect that you expect your partner to return? To work toward the mutual benefit of both partners, every partnership—whether business or personal—needs to meet all three major criteria addressed in these questions: commitment, common goals, and communication.

If you answered no to any of these questions, it signals an area that you need to address immediately to improve your relationship. Still, if you are both willing to put in the time and effort needed to improve your relationship, you will soon answer yes to all these questions. As you both work toward Mutual Partnership, you may want to repeat this exercise periodically to mark your progress. With each step of relationship recovery, you will find that your yesses resound with greater and greater conviction.

As you will discover in striving to improve your intimate bonds, relationships in recovery demand the same commitment and vigilance that personal recovery does. By now, you know that your individual recovery program will not work successfully for you unless you are completely willing to work on *making* it successful through perseverance and practice. Just as your individual sanity, sobriety, and serenity depend on your commitment to go to any lengths to ensure them, so does the success of your relationships. In short, you need to be just as committed to relationship recovery as you are to your personal recovery.

The recovery of your relationship, because it involves more than just you, depends on your work as a team. If you are the only one who is committed to recovery or to improving your relationship, you will find it impossible to make mutual changes in your relationship. Your relationships—even the one with the alcoholic—will still get better as you pursue your personal recovery. But your relationship with the alcoholic can never completely recover unless he or she joins you in a mutual commitment to improve yourselves and your partnership. If only one of you is willing to change, it makes little sense to try to work as a team on your relationship. On the other hand, if both of you make a commitment to work on recovery, on yourselves, and on your relationship, then your relationship has a chance to begin to work for you.

Of course, mutual commitment to recovery, in itself, will not make all your relationship problems disappear—any more than your devotion to individual improvement made your personal problems vanish. You will undoubtedly need to confront breakdowns of communication, conflicts that demand resolution for the partnership to survive, disagreements, and even fights with your partner. If you are involved in a romantic relationship with the alcoholic in your life, there's a good chance that you will encounter difficulties tied to your mutual sexuality and intimacy. Finally, once you have improved your relationship with the recovering alcoholic, you may still have work to do on other relationships that are important to you: with your children, other family members, and friends.

The following chapters address these most common difficulties of relationships in recovery. By working to overcome these obstacles, you will gain a new perspective on your relationships as you improve them. You will learn strategies that will improve your communication and strengthen your commitment, making it easier and more fulfilling to work toward common goals. Although the range of specific problems you may encounter in *your* relationships is infinite, you will know that you can apply the general problem-solving guidelines you learn here to any particular difficulty you meet.

After the long trail of illness, the recovery of your relationships will not be easy. It will demand a lot of TLC on the part of everyone involved in the relationship. Traditionally, TLC stands for tender, loving care, but in the case of relationships in recovery, TLC also refers to talking, listening, and commitment. Mutual commitment is the cornerstone of any healthy partnership, the cement that holds people together and makes the work involved in building a relationship worthwhile. Talking openly and honestly and listening with just as much openness and freedom from prejudice or preconception are at the heart of productive communication, the kind of interaction that contributes to the growth of people and their relationships. A favorite slogan from AA and Al-Anon states, "Together We Can." When everyone involved in a partnership— both people in an intimate relationship or all members of a family—practice both kinds of TLC, "Together We Can" becomes more than a slogan, more than a mere possibility; it becomes the reality of the relationship.

NEW PERSPECTIVES, NEW COMMITMENT

"I was never really committed to any woman before I got sober," admits Ralph, a forty-eight-year-old writer who divorced after a ten-year marriage. A year after his divorce, he joined AA and started to sober up. That was fifteen years ago. "The other night I counted up how many women I'd had some kind of romantic involvement with since I came into the program: forty-six women. That wasn't during my wild drinking days, mind you, but *after*, when I had supposedly straightened up my act. At least that's what I told myself. . . .

"In all my attachments, there seemed to be some sort of

unspoken agreement that whatever happened was an interlude. For a long time, I thought I'd just keep adding to that list and take it out when I was seventy-five and chuckle a bit. But I never really got close to any of those women, and there was always an undercurrent of loneliness beneath my braggadocio. I was like the mysterious stranger, passing through town, but never stopping anywhere for very long. And it seemed clear to me, and to these women, that that was the way it was always going to be.

"My relationships, if they even deserve the name, fell into three patterns. First, 'friends, then fall into bed'; second, 'passion, and maybe friendship later'; and finally, 'infatuation,' in which I would never initiate anything, even though I was very attracted to someone. If anything happened in that sort of relationship, it was only because the woman pursued and caught me. But no matter which pattern I followed, the result was always the same. After a pretty short time, I'd find some way to end the relationship."

Despite the relative safety they offer, purely casual, superficial relationships are largely unsatisfying for most people. Most people want to move beyond superficiality to build substantive, *intimate* relationships. Yet the patterns of interaction that become habitual when alcoholism and codependency are in full swing actually block intimacy. To prevent anyone from discovering their "awful secret," active alcoholics and codependents routinely keep people at a distance. While these illnesses ruled, the only close connections formed with others were based on mutual secrecy, which prevented any sort of commitment founded on mutual honesty. And if ignored, these habitual patterns of interaction—or, more accurately, avoidance of any meaningful interaction—may persist for months or even years after recovery. Ralph needed more than fifteen years in AA before he felt ready to make a commitment to build a truly intimate relationship for the first time in his life.

"When I met Cindy, everything changed," Ralph explains. "I fell in love. For the first time in my life, I actually told a woman that I love her, that I want to have a home with her and a family. I'd never taken a risk like that with anyone before, but I'm just not afraid I'm going to get socked in the jaw or rejected by her.

"I'm not about to give this relationship up. I hope it lasts forever, but no matter how long it lasts—weeks, months, or years—I'm there for the duration. I'm committed to Cindy whatever happens. I feel we're in this together and it feels great.

"With Cindy, I feel like I'm finally being true to myself; I'm not selling myself short anymore. Maybe that's what commitment is all about—being 'fiercely honest' with yourself and with another person. I'd heard that expression in the program before, but I never really knew what it meant. But now, that's how I feel. I'm through not being the person I want to be. Now I have a whole different perspective. With Cindy, I feel we're starting with a clean slate, and at the top of that slate is the word commitment."

Like most recovering alcoholics and codependents, Ralph needed to do a great deal of self-exploration before he was ready to commit himself truly to another person. Before initiating his Pioneering work of self-discovery, Ralph confesses, he really didn't know what he wanted, aside from maintaining his sobriety. But the process of taking a thorough and honest look at himself allowed Ralph to bring more honesty into his relationship with others. Unless you know who you are and what you want and need, you cannot communicate these discoveries to someone else. And since this sort of primal communication is essential to being truly understood and accepted by another person and to getting those needs met, you cannot build any real commitment without it.

For Ralph, it took fifteen years to become honest enough with himself to know that he wanted more intimate relationships. Like Ralph, you may just now be moving toward a more committed relationship and true intimacy, no matter how long you and your partner have been in recovery. But whether you have only recently entered a new relationship or you are attempting to rebuild one that has already seen a long history of illness, pain, and recovery, you should feel confident of your ability to create a Mutual Partnership. As an accomplished Pioneer, you have plenty of self-knowledge and experience that will contribute to the growth of any relationship. Whether the relationship is old or new, there's a new *you* in the relationship. And by bringing this new understanding of yourself to bear in your personal relationships, you will have a new perspective about your partnership and life in general. As you stand at the threshold of the Mutual-Partner stage of recovery, are you, like Ralph, looking for more commitment and intimacy? Do you know what you want and need from others? If you don't, you still have some work to do on the Pioneer stage of recovery.

As Ralph discovered, you need a solid sense of self to commit yourself to a relationship. If you have developed a solid sense of self through your work as a Pioneer, you should be able to affirm all the following statements as true:

1. I affirm my beliefs, values, and opinions.
2. I focus on changing myself, not my partner.
3. I understand the ways in which I am like and unlike my partner and I appreciate these individual qualities.
4. I don't feel it necessary to try to become the person my partner wants me to be—unless that's the person who *I* want to be.
5. I accept and respect my partner for being herself or himself.

If you can repeat all these statements aloud and truly believe them, then you have developed a solid sense of yourself—and yourself in relationship to others. You are prepared to enter or work toward a committed and intimate Mutual Partnership.

WHEN "I" AND "YOU" BECOME "WE"

Mutual Partnerships require the dedication of both partners to working together to achieve common goals. Thus, to improve your relationship in recovery, you will need to confront problems as a team. In Mutual Partnerships, problems are no longer solely "yours" or "mine," but "ours."

"But wait a second!" you may object. "What happened to the principle of detachment?" You've worked hard to develop your ability to practice detachment in the first two stages of recovery. Since most codependents (and many alcoholics) have a tendency to overinvolve themselves in other people's problems and take on other people's burdens, you *needed* to practice detachment to develop and master that skill. And you will never lose that ability to detach yourself from other people's problems—even while you attempt to reattach or form new attachments. But now you need to shift gears—to approach relationship problems as a team.

Obviously, there will be times when you will need to address certain problems on your own, individually, and times when your partner will need to do the same. Sometimes you will need to take sole responsibility for resolving a personal problem. At other times (and for many, this challenge is an even more demanding one), you will need to relegate all responsibility, respecting your partner's ability to handle her or his own difficulties. But most of the time, you will be in the "partnership business." Being in the partnership business means that whenever any problem affects or involves your relationship or both of you as individuals, you will need to try to solve the difficulty together. You and your partner need to agree that arbitrary, one-sided decisions will not be allowed in any question that involves a mutual concern. Now that you're both more secure in your individual recovery programs, to improve your relationship, you need to commit yourselves to staying connected and to solving your problems mutually, as partners.

If you have gotten used to making a lot of decisions on your own, as you needed to do in the Eye-Opener and Pioneer stages of recovery, you may think that this move from detachment to reattachment seems like a difficult adjustment. But though it may surprise you, the shift from detachment back to a secure attachment will not be such a radical change. After all, you've depended on a Higher Power or those involved in your recovery program or both to get this far. And through your advice and encouragement, you've helped others in your recovery program to overcome their problems, too. So all along, while detaching yourself from problems that truly belong to another person, you've been attaching yourself to others.

Although it may feel a little uncomfortable at first, allow yourself to practice attachment once again. Have confidence in your knowledge of interpersonal boundaries; you know how to distinguish between a challenge that truly involves you and something that is solely your partner's problem. You've developed a solid sense of self now, one that won't get lost in your relationships.

The decision to commit yourself to being part of a "we" relationship does not mean abandoning your individual identities as "you" and "me." Because you each have your separate perspectives, you may have serious disagreements. Since you have committed yourself to a Mutual Partnership, however, even when you argue most strongly, you have mutually promised each other that you will do your best to prevent this disparity from damaging the stability of your relationship. This commitment to a Mutual Partnership does not mean total, uninterrupted harmony. It simply means that you have pledged yourselves to approaching difficulties as a team. And in doing so, you have each recognized the possibility that two people can accomplish much more together than either person could do alone.

This possibility can indeed become a reality. The consolidated front of Mutual Partnership offers a much stronger position from which to tackle problems. Because two heads really are better than one, you have doubled your resources by relying on each other. You can grow individually—and grow closer together—by opening yourself up to the perspective of another person. If you and your partner are both in recovery, however, gaining access to each other's perspectives will require you to get to know each other all over again.

"Even though Laura and I have been married for a dozen years, it's only in recent months that we've felt like real partners," confesses Cal, who joined Al-Anon two years ago, when his wife joined AA. "I did marry her, but I still don't think I ever made a real commitment. I remember thinking on our wedding day that she was a wonderful person, and I liked her very much. But I couldn't have told you why we were getting married.

"Getting to know each other in recovery has been like going back to our early dating days. We were unsure of ourselves and each other. It took many months and a lot of recovery for both of us to trust again. After putting in a lot of time and work, we both know now that we are in a partnership. We support each other instead of trying to control each other the way we did in the past. We own up to our flaws and confront our problems together instead of ignoring them or blaming them on the other person. We still don't agree about everything. But when we disagree, we don't talk at each other anymore; we listen to each other. We're on the same team, rather than on opposing teams, and it feels good to have that kind of attitude. We're so much more committed to each other today than we were the day we got married. Now we know what commitment really means."

Cal and Laura have become Mutual Partners in recovery. In their commitment to pursue their common goals as a team, they have demonstrated their mutual faith in their ability to work things out together as best as they can. Together, they are working on building honesty, trust, commitment, support, and communication—the essential ingredients of a Mutual Partnership.

Like all Mutual Partners, Laura and Cal are striving for a new sense of balance in their relationship. You, too, will need to struggle to find the proper balance between separateness and togetherness, detachment and attachment, distance and closeness. This sense of balance, combining a solid "me" with a solid "we," is the mark of true intimacy. Intimacy demands that you neither sacrifice yourself to maintain your relationships nor sacrifice your relationships to maintain a strong identity. This balance—the ability to continue to develop an individual sense of self while remaining emotionally connected to others—will best promote your growth as individuals and as a team.

Have you begun to develop the sense of balance essential to true intimacy as Mutual Partners? If you have made even a tentative start, then you can begin working toward some common goals. Do you and your partner share common goals in your relationship? Write down some of the goals you hope to achieve with your partner or through your relationship and ask your partner to do the same. Your goals may be specific—for instance, learning to dance together or being able to afford a new car. Or they may be general—for example, increasing your love for each other or helping each other grow. By sharing these goals with each other, you will discover objectives you already have in common. If you are willing to embrace each other's goals, you will build new common goals.

Marta and Howard did this exercise together and came up with the following lists:

MARTA'S GOALS

Increasing the warm feelings we feel toward each other
Being honest with each other
Rearing happy, healthy children
Moving out of the city
Buying a new car
Building a relationship in which we can both grow

HOWARD'S GOALS

Loving each other more every day
Sharing our love with our children
Buying a house in the country

Planning an enormous family reunion
Feeling comfortable with each other
Continuing our recovery

Howard and Marta discovered that many of their ambitions were similar. Both wanted to see their love grow, to advance their recovery, to contribute to their children's happiness and well-being, and to move out of their city apartment. In addition, they both decided to add one of the other's goals to their individual lists. Howard agreed that he would like their relationship to become more honest, while Marta shared her husband's desire for a comfortable relationship. Even when they disagreed with each other's goals, Howard and Marta discovered that it was okay to do so. Howard, for one, loved his old car and did not think they really needed a new one. And Marta, for her part, did not share her husband's wish to organize a big family reunion. She was concerned about exposing their children to the possible "bad influence" of Howard's brothers, both of whom were active alcoholics. Since they did not share these aims, they agreed to put them aside temporarily and to devote themselves to attaining their common goals instead.

If you discover that you share common coals with your partner, discuss ways in which you can try to achieve them together. Whatever specific goals you both decide to pursue in your relationship, make sure you are both committed to aiming toward the general goals of Mutual Partnership as well. Both of you should regularly affirm the following statements, which spell out the ingredients needed to balance a strong sense of self and a strong relationship.

1. I acknowledge and share my strengths and vulnerabilities and encourage my partner to do likewise.
2. I confront, rather than run away from, difficult problems in our relationship.
3. I am committed to working out a problem together, rather than insisting on getting my own way.

4. In working out problems together, I set priorities and stick to my own bottom line when we cannot compromise on a vital issue.
5. I communicate as openly and honestly as I can.

In attempting to attain these standards, remind yourself—and each other—that you don't have to be perfect. As long as you continually and sincerely aim toward these ideals and make some progress together, you are on the right track.

Movement toward Mutual Partnership involves teamwork. And this teamwork, in itself, will draw you closer together. Your mutual awareness, identification of problems, and efforts to meet challenges together will feed your intimacy and commitment to each other. As a Pioneer, you advanced your personal recovery by getting to know yourself better. Similarly, by exploring and understanding your relationship more fully, you will move toward greater intimacy and love as partners—whether the two of you are husband and wife, lovers, friends, siblings, or parent and adult child. The combination of teamwork and understanding almost inevitably increases intimacy and mutual commitment. And the more work you put in together, the more satisfying results you will achieve with your labor of love.

7

OPENNESS AND HONESTY

The Keys to Communication

As a rule, whenever alcoholism and codependency are active in a relationship or a family, most people find it difficult, if not impossible, to be honest. Denial, covering up, and the avoidance of all problems become habitual. This pattern of dishonesty perpetuates itself—and the illness—in the relationship. When you were involved in an alcoholic relationship, you no doubt felt you had to protect yourself and your loved ones. And this understandable wish to keep everything under a tight lid made it hard to risk being honest and open in your everyday communication. The desire to avoid conflict and to keep tensions under control, for example, may have prompted you to try to "people-please," to do and say what you guessed other people wanted you to do and say instead of what you wanted. But since you thought it necessary to present a "false self" to the outside world, you started to feel that people would never like you as you really were. Because you avoided rigorous honesty with yourself and with others, you unwittingly damaged your self-esteem.

If you are like most people in recovery, however, you want to stop playing these dishonest games. You have a new and powerful desire to be completely honest with yourself and others. As a Pioneer, you worked to discover your "true self"—work that will continue for the rest of your life. Now, as a Mutual Partner, you probably want to present that self truly to other people. You now know that you can change those old patterns that were built on a foundation of lying and deceit. All it takes is a little practice—the kind of practice that rarely is done in alcoholic relationships. If you want to be as honest with others as you are with yourself, you *can* be.

OPEN COMMUNICATION NOW, NOT LATER

For most of us, our current ability to be honest is rooted in what we learned as children. Parents and siblings teach children many dos and don'ts regarding communication—rules that spell out exactly what family members can and cannot discuss. And we tend to carry these old rules into all our new relationships. (Indeed, the rules of communication we learned in our families often mimic the dos and don'ts that our parents learned in *their* childhood homes.) Various "Don't Talk" rules exist in many families, but especially those with lingering illnesses or chronic problems like alcoholism, gambling, or other compulsive behaviors. Were any of the following rules observed in your childhood home?

1. Don't tell . . . (about the family secret).
2. Don't talk about your feelings.
3. Don't show affection.
4. Don't talk about sex.
5. Don't be angry.
6. Don't confront anyone.
7. Don't disagree.
8. Don't show your vulnerabilities.
9. Don't admit you're afraid.
10. Don't ask for help.

11. Don't let anyone know you made a mistake.
12. Don't say you're sorry.

Can you add more rules to this list, rules you learned while you were growing up? Do they contribute to patterns of noncommunication in your present relationship or relationships?

Unfortunately, if you and your partner continue to observe these old Don't Talk rules, which prohibit the honest sharing of feelings and the development of mutual intimacy, your relationship will never truly recover. When people refuse to talk openly and honestly, they "pressure cook" their emotions. Unexpressed feelings, needs, and opinions cause tension to build up, creating more and more pressure until the tension finally explodes. If directed inward, this explosion may induce severe depression and feelings of helplessness. If directed outward, the violent outburst can precipitate a major "fallout," further cementing patterns of noncommunication and perhaps creating irreconcilable differences.

But you don't have to live by these old, outmoded rules of communication forever. Sit down with your partner and discuss which Don't Talk rules you both lived by—the rules that still stand in the way of open and honest communication today. Also discuss those rules of communication that just one of you lived by. You may have lived by one rule and expected your partner, who perhaps lived by a different rule, to do the same. These mismatched rules of communication may have created unspoken conflict between you. After examining these Don't Talk rules, work together to decide which rules you want to change to improve your communication today. To strengthen your Mutual Partnership, you need to work together to develop *new* methods of communication that will increase your intimacy and understanding of each other.

In itself, this exercise will help to overcome patterns of noncommunication by initiating honesty and openness. You need to practice this kind of honesty, teaching yourself to use open communication as a "pressure valve" by saying what you feel at the moment. When you learn to say what bothers you when it bothers you, for instance, you avoid burdening your relationship with a pile of unspoken resentments and tension. But there is a risk involved in this kind of openness. You may fear that others will react to any honest expression of your thoughts and feelings—especially doubts, reservations, criticism, or other "negative" opinions—with disapproval or rejection.

Stan and Virginia, recovering alcoholics who attend both AA and Al-Anon meetings, shared this fear of disapproval or rejection. After dating for less than a year, they started coming to me for couples counseling. They each voiced concern about the other's tendency to withdraw emotionally or physically from any hint of tension in their relationship. They kept their feelings all bottled up because of their fear of rejection. But they each experienced the other person's silence as "devastating." They were terrified that the disapproval and rejection implied by this silence indicated that their relationship was over. And, in fact, their mutual silence was creating greater and greater distance between them.

After practicing open communication during several couples-counseling sessions, Virginia and Stan realized that whenever any tension surfaced in their relationship, they both reacted by following a similar pattern. Any critical—or even questioning—remark tended to set off the following progression of feelings:

1. A sense of disapproval from another person indicates this person will abandon me.
2. I am afraid of abandonment, so I'd better leave this relationship first.
3. I will withdraw in silence.
4. Now that I've "left," I don't have to worry about the other person leaving *me*.

This pattern had persisted in all their relationships in the past. Virginia confessed that her relationships had never lasted more than three months. And though Stan had been married several times, he admitted that he had always withdrawn emotionally from his wives. Their powerful fears of abandonment had made it impossible for either Virginia or Stan to stay in any relationship for long.

Stan and Virginia had come close to breaking up themselves several times, but they stayed together despite their urge to flee. Fortunately, their relationship with each other meant enough to them so that they sought help to overcome their difficulties. In the course of counseling, they realized that their impulse to withdraw was based on a false premise: "If you love me, you'll agree with everything I say and do. If you disagree or disapprove of anything I say or do, that means you don't love me and you'll leave me." They needed to recognize that expressions of disappointment, disapproval, anger, or annoyance do not always signal the doom and gloom of separation. Indeed, sometimes we feel angriest at those people whom we love the most.

Once Virginia and Stan saw that equating love with total agreement and approval was a fallacy, they became less poised for flight. They understood—and clearly expressed to each other—that giving voice to feelings like anger, frustration, or disappointment did not signal a lack of love. As they worked to make their communication more open, they slowly became more comfortable with expressing negative feelings and hearing these feelings expressed without thinking that they were unloved or unlovable.

"It's a big relief for me to know that I don't have to be perfect and that this will never be the 'perfect relationship' I'd always hoped for," acknowledges Virginia. "We're trying to make each other feel comfortable with disagreement, so we both feel we can be open with each other. We know now that when things go wrong, it doesn't mean the relationship is doomed. It just means we have to work harder to get ourselves back on the same track. Having differences doesn't mean we have to withdraw. Just because we disagree doesn't mean we're bad, wrong, or rejected."

Contrary to our romantic ideals, no relationship in the real world exists without some difficulties. But, as you know from the history of alcoholism in your relationship or relationships, these problems won't disappear just because you refuse to talk about them. By committing yourself to the honesty necessary for a Mutual Partnership, however, you will gain the opportunity to work through these problems together. If both you and your partner can openly share your feelings, even uncomfortable feelings, you can then work together to turn the wrongs of your relationship into rights.

Intimacy develops between two people through this free exchange of all feelings—positive and negative. But if you want ot encourage intimacy in your relationship, you will have to keep the lines of communication open. Like Stan and Virginia, you and your partner may not only need to give yourselves permission to feel your negative feelings, but you may need to give each other permission to express these feelings. However, this permission will be short lived and do little good unless each of you learns to express honest emotion without hostility or fear. You may both need to practice expressing anger, frustration, and disappointment in ways that neither attack nor blame each other.

At the same time, you will need to work on your willingness to listen carefully, affirming your partner's rights to negative feelings without becoming overly defensive or reacting with an attack on your partner. If you remain open to it, you will discover that another person's honest opinion offers you a new perspective on your life. Often, an honest exchange of feelings and thoughts may point to areas of yourself or your relationship that need some work. You may want to do some soul-searching or some exploration of your relationship in response to your partner's observation or expression of emotion. And even if ultimately you disagree with what your partner has said, an honest exchange of opposing views need not destroy your relationship, as Virginia and Stan happily discovered.

If you both work to improve your communication, you will no longer have to fear each other's anger or disapproval. If you can leave behind the attack-defense mode of expression that actually stands in the way of productive communication, your mutual openness and honesty can help improve your relationship in recovery. Through practice and mutual support, you can develop habits of honest sharing and receptive listening that will help you grow as individuals and as partners. And by verbalizing your feelings without attacking your partner, you can not only expel them in a nonharmful manner, but move toward enhanced mutual understanding and intimacy.

The rewards of intimacy, reaped through open and honest communication, are well worth any risk of disapproval or rejection. Although openness may initially create a distance between you and another person, you need to present your true self to foster intimacy. Without this kind of honest interaction, you have no chance to get close to anyone else. Mutual honesty —sharing both positive and negative thoughts and emotions— creates strong bonds between people. By communicating your deepest fears and feelings, as Virginia and Stan found out, you can help each other overcome your fears and change the old patterns that have stood in the way of intimacy in the past. And this realization can help strengthen your commitment to honesty, intimacy, and each other.

COMMUNICATION, NOT CLAIRVOYANCE

In some cases, you may not openly say what you are feeling because you think your partner already knows—or at least, *should* know—what you are thinking or feeling. Similarly, you may *think* you know what your partner is thinking or feeling, on the basis of your previous experiences with him or her, and therefore may not bother to ask. Often, for instance, couples assume that they agree with each other without actually checking out their impressions. Unfortunately, this reliance on clairvoyance instead of communication is one of the most frequent causes of misunderstanding in intimate relationships. Even in the closest relationships, mind reading of this sort is nothing better than educated guesswork. And no matter how educated, guesswork regularly leads to mistakes and misunderstandings.

Larry, an actor, and Kim, a high-powered lawyer, have been dating for over a year. Larry regularly attends AA meetings, and both of them receive individual and couples counseling. Recently, shortly after they had started to talk about the possibility of marriage, they had to overcome a misunderstanding that threatened to drive them apart, a breach created by an episode of mutual mind reading. While driving home after a visit to some old friends of Kim's, Kim asked Larry whether he was satisfied with his career. Larry didn't say anything in response; instead he withdrew emotionally and silently drove Kim home. Kim interpreted this withdrawal as a rejection of her and assumed that he wanted to continue his "single" lifestyle, rather than get married. For a full week, neither of them talked and, as they later shared with each other, both assumed the relationship was "over."

Finally, Kim took the initiative to try to clear things up. She called Larry and told him she had scheduled a couples therapy session to try to deal with the barrier that had suddenly sprung up between them. In the safety of my office, Larry revealed that he had felt uncomfortable and intimidated by the grand lifestyle of Kim's old friends. So when Kim asked him about his career, Larry assumed that she was comparing her friends' lifestyle with his and judging him a failure. Already feeling like an outsider, he now felt like he wasn't good enough for her, that his career didn't measure up to her "high standards."

Kim used the couples session to correct Larry's mind *mis*-reading. She made it clear that she didn't care how much money he made. But she had noticed that he seemed torn between performing in a musical, teaching acting, and trying to produce a play, and she wanted to make sure he was happy with the work he was doing. When he stopped to listen to what Kim was *really* saying, he realized she had a point. He decided to rethink his priorities and find a way to focus his energy on producing, the part of his work that he liked doing the most.

Kim and Larry misread each other because they both tried to read the other's mind and because they both encouraged the other to attempt this guesswork. Kim said little in their conversation in the car, and Larry said nothing. Then instead of exploring the problem that had suddenly silenced them, they both just let the subject die. Instead of communicating further, they tried to guess what the other was thinking and feeling. And in assuming that they understood each other, both Kim and Larry ended up misunderstanding each other's messages.

If you want to avoid this kind of misunderstanding, don't resort to mind reading and don't force your partner to rely on guesswork by shutting up completely, closing off all avenues of communication. Observe the three basic rules that prevent mind reading:

1. Honestly communicate your thoughts and feelings as fully as you can.
2. Don't assume anything about your partner's thoughts or feelings.
3. When in doubt, check it out. Ask your partner to share what she or he is feeling or thinking.

Whenever you sense some feeling or motivation underlying your partner's words or actions, don't simply accept that your assumption is right. Don't try to reach a verdict based on inconclusive evidence. That's what Larry did at first, in assuming that Kim considered him a failure. And Kim did likewise, guessing that Larry had rejected her for the single life. Fortunately, in thinking it over, Kim allowed the possibility that she had misunderstood him. And this acknowledgment of imperfection led to a happy ending for Larry and Kim. If you have made an assumption about your partner's emotions or motives, don't let it end there. Check out your impressions instead of checking out of the relationship. Share your impressions with your partner and ask if they're right. Explore these feelings—or your interpretation of these feelings—together, as a team. Through honest and open communication, you, too, can clear up misunderstandings and give your story a happy ending.

HONESTY: THE BEST POLICY (MOST OF THE TIME)

Al-Anon's and AA's policy of "rigorous honesty" is an excellent ideal. But the ideal sometimes doesn't work in practice. As you work on your recovering relationship, both you and your partner will need to put this ideal to the test in many different circumstances. You will need to ask yourself, "Is rigorous honesty *always* the best policy? How honest is *too* honest?"

You may, for instance, have kept a secret from someone close to you for a long time and now want to reveal yourself fully. Certainly, this new honesty will relieve you of the burden of secrecy. But if you are motivated solely by the desire to get out from under this weight, reconsider the appropriateness of your honesty. If relieving yourself of the burden of secrecy places an unfair burden on someone else, don't do it. Stop and think about your motivation and the consequences of your honesty before saying anything. Remind yourself that it's wrong to try to buy your peace of mind at the expense of those around you.

The Ninth Step of AA and Al-Anon offers some sound practical advice in this regard. "Made direct amends to such people whenever possible, *except when to do so would injure them or others.*" This cautionary note on making amends applies just as much to the question of complete honesty. Complete disclosure, purely in the name of "rigorous honesty," cannot justify inflicting unnecessary emotional pain on the people who are close to you. If you are in a situation in which the honesty you are considering may harm another person, check your motives and your timing first before disclosing anything.

George, a client of mine who had been attending AA for three years, had recently become engaged. But he told me in a counseling session that he was suddenly "struck gaga" by all the young and beautiful women he saw on the street. Against this backdrop of attractive women, George started to think that Ann, his fiancée, looked a little drab in comparison. In struggling to live up to AA's standard of "rigorous honesty," George wanted to know whether he should tell Ann how much prettier he thought other women were. Almost everyone would agree that this is obviously a situation in which it would be best *not* to tell the truth.

I encouraged George to look at himself with the same critical eye he had been applying to Ann's appearance. I asked him to consider why, just after getting engaged, he suddenly found other women so attractive. Upon introspection, he realized that in complaining about Ann's physical attractiveness, he was trying to justify his own doubts and fears regarding marriage. Because he doubted his ability to be intimate, he had started to panic about his engagement. He came to see that if he had told Ann that he found her unattractive compared to other women, he would have hurt her and would have created an enormous distance between them, one that might have led to their breakup. He realized that although this outcome would have eased his immediate fear of intimacy, he wanted to work on overcoming this fear in a more constructive and permanent way through counseling. He decided that he wanted to build intimate relationships instead of always running away from them.

As George realized, "But that's the truth . . ." does not let you off the hook in deciding whether to speak out or remain silent. The mere fact that you are being honest is never a good excuse for inflicting unnecessary harm on someone else. Recognizing that some types of honesty actually inhibit or destroy intimacy rather than promote it, remember to explore the purity of your motivations first. Make sure that you are impelled to tell the truth primarily by the ideal of honesty and the goal of building Mutual Partnerships in your relationships. Don't use your honesty as an excuse to push other people away, as George almost did, or to hurt them in any way.

Just as "rigorous honesty" cannot be used as an excuse to

hurt someone, however, the fact that the truth may hurt your partner should not *in itself* be used as an excuse to *avoid* telling the truth. Naturally, the truth sometimes hurts; but lying or continuing a pattern of dishonesty sometimes hurts even more. In these cases, even though honesty will hurt, it is still necessary. For this reason, in considering what to reveal, you may have to weigh which hurts more: truth or silence? So if you want to be totally honest with your partner, make sure you are being totally honest with yourself first.

Before you tell the whole truth, ask yourself:

1. What do I hope to accomplish by revealing this truth?
2. What are the possible consequences of my disclosure?
3. Will revealing this truth hurt the person I tell?
4. Will revealing this truth hurt a third person?
5. Do I have the right to involve a third person?
6. If I know that some of the details are unnecessary and may be harmful, is it possible to tell this truth without revealing every little detail about it?

Before you decide to remain silent, ask yourself:

1. Will keeping this truth secret harm the other person?
2. If that person inadvertently learned my "secret," would he or she be most hurt by my failure to be open and honest?
3. Will this particular secret make it impossible for us to make honesty the cornerstone of a Mutual Partnership in this relationship?
4. Is this secret an isolated incident or part of a pattern of dishonesty on my part?
5. How would I feel if the other person had this secret and didn't tell me?
6. How is my ego tied up with my secret? Am I worried about how the other person will see me if I expose myself in this way?

7. Have I decided to avoid doing the honest thing, simply to escape the personal consequences of my actions?

These are by no means easy questions, but answering them will reinforce your understanding that your actions and your honesty have consequences—not just in their impact on you, but in their effect on others and on your relationship with them. If, after answering all these questions, you are still not sure about whether and how to tell this truth, you may find it helpful to discuss it with your sponsor, therapist, or spiritual adviser. In practice, deciding whether to speak out or remain silent about a particular feeling, thought, or experience can become extremely complicated. Since many different factors are inevitably involved in such decisions, an outside perspective can sometimes shed new light on specific applications of rigorous honesty.

Marybeth and Nelson, clients who see me for both individual and couples counseling, have both been in AA and Al-Anon for four years. In recovery, their level of commitment and their ability to be honest with each other have increased dramatically. But one big secret still weighed on Nelson's mind: During his drinking days, he had had several one-night stands at the same time he was dating Marybeth.

Marybeth had given him opportunities to reveal his secret, but he had never taken advantage of them. Because she had some vague suspicions, she had asked him several times whether he had been faithful to her during their courtship. And though she had assured him that she just wanted to know the truth and that she would not be judgmental about it, he had steadfastly maintained the "lie" of his fidelity. Yet the more sobriety Nelson attained, the more unhappy he felt with this secret that threatened their relationship.

When he brought the subject up in one of our individual counseling sessions, I suggested that in addition to weighing the relative harm of honesty and secrecy with me, he should also talk it over with his AA sponsor. Nelson gave this issue serious thought before reaching a decision. Ultimately, he decided that he could no longer build a foundation of honesty in the rest of his relationship while holding on to this lie. He realized that his secretiveness was hurting him and restricting the intimacy of his relationship with Marybeth and that continuing to lie would hurt her even more than would finally telling the truth. With guidance and support from his sponsor and me, Nelson decided that in this case, honesty would indeed be the best policy. Even though he knew it would hurt her and make her angry, he had to tell Marybeth about his past infidelity.

Despite feeling certain that he was doing the "right thing," Nelson had some second thoughts after the fact. Marybeth was indeed furious at him, and they fought about it for three days. In their next couples session, Nelson claimed that he felt "manipulated" by her previous assurances that she would not be judgmental. Marybeth admitted that when she was pressuring Nelson to tell her the truth, she did not realize how shocked, disappointed, and angry she would feel when he told her. But she also made Nelson see that she was entitled to feel "betrayed." She insisted that although the truth hurt, she was more upset that Nelson had lied to her for so many years than that he had had some affairs before she and he had made a real commitment to each other.

Nelson acknowledged that Marybeth had every right to be upset about his trail of lies. He realized how important honesty was to Marybeth and apologized again for his inability to tell the truth to her earlier. Nelson confessed that ever since his teenage years, when both his parents had died, he has suffered from a powerful fear of abandonment. Because he loved Marybeth so much, Nelson was always afraid of losing her. In his drinking days and his first years of sobriety, he still felt too insecure and distrusting to risk being honest. He admitted that he had needed to become more secure about himself, his recovery, and his relationship with Marybeth before he felt he could take the risk and accept the responsibility of being more open, honest, and trusting.

There was no easy "right" answer about whether to tell the

truth in this situation, but Nelson and Marybeth had to consider what was right for them. In retrospect, despite the emotional upheaval it caused, both Marybeth and Nelson agreed that Nelson had done the right thing in finally choosing to tell her. Though initially it created excruciating pain for both of them, Marybeth and Nelson felt relieved that the truth had finally been told. For Marybeth, the truth hurt, but it still felt better than the suspicions that had nagged her all along.

A dark cloud had been hanging over their relationship for years. When the cloud burst, a huge storm followed, but when the storm died down, the cloud disappeared. The fight had cleared the air, once and for all. After discussing it in couples counseling for several weeks, they agreed to put the matter to rest for good. They made a mutual commitment to practice open and honest communication with each other. And because they had learned a lot about themselves and about each other, they felt closer than they ever had before.

If you are trying to decide whether to speak out or remain silent regarding a particular issue in your Mutual Partnership, there may be no simple "right" answer in your case either. Nevertheless, there are lots of "right" questions that can help you determine the right course in your relationship as you move toward an honest Mutual Partnership. If you follow the guidelines outlined earlier in exploring your motivations and considering the possible consequences of your revelation, you will probably reach a sound decision about what to reveal and what not to reveal.

MOVING FROM DISHONEST IDEALISM TO HONEST REALISM

As a Pioneer, self-honesty required you to take a good hard look at yourself, to destroy the myths and misconceptions you had about yourself. Similarly, honesty in any Mutual Partnership demands that you examine that relationship thoroughly and recognize the reality of what's involved. Rigorous honesty in a Mutual Partnership requires a realistic appraisal of yourself, the other person, and the relationship.

Unfortunately, such a rigorous appraisal is easier said than done in the first years of recovery. No matter what their particular relationship, two people in early recovery, like couples in the first year of a romance, often view their relationship through rose-colored glasses. Since recovery has transformed each of you into a "new" person, you have indeed entered into a new relationship. And in the flush of early recovery, just as in the beginning of a romance, a pink cloud of idealism may linger overhead, obscuring the real nature of both people and of the relationship. The other person—whether a parent, a lover, a spouse, a sibling, or a friend—may look like some kind of superhero now that he or she has "taken care of" the problem of addiction or codependency.

New partners discover new truths about each other all the time, however. When looked at clearly and closely, our heroes rarely live up to our high expectations. And the destruction of the pink clouds, false myths, and unrealizable ideals of relationships in recovery can be painful and discouraging. As perceptions move from idealistic hopes to realistic and honest assessments, it's natural to have disappointments. As you work on becoming more honest in your Mutual Partnership, you will need to work on reconciling the disappointments that will inevitably come as you open your eyes to the reality of your relationship in recovery.

"We got married in early recovery, and so we thought we were a very special couple. We thought we could have this perfect marriage, since we were both sober and both working our recovery programs," remembers Nelson, reflecting on his early deception and later honesty regarding his one-night stands. "Marybeth and I felt we had an edge that most people don't have. We thought we wouldn't have the same kinds of problems with our relationship that we saw other people having.

"Telling my secret really blew that out of the water. I wasn't too happy about being knocked off my pedestal. I was no longer perfect, and neither was our relationship. But I can see now that the myth we had created about our relationship was unrealistic and very unhealthy. We were being dishonest with ourselves, kidding ourselves.

"Now that I've shattered the myth of the perfect couple, I hope we won't be so devastated when we see that we have problems like everyone else. We're starting to recognize that we really do have some problems, but at the same time we're learning how to work out those problems. We know that getting honest and staying honest aren't always going to be easy. But they finally feel right."

Building relationships, like recovery itself, is a developmental process. As Nelson and Marybeth discovered, the honesty required to build a Mutual Partnership can sometimes be painful and disappointing. But the "ideal relationship" they had created was based on closed eyes and less-than-open communication. Nelson knew all along that his courtship had been based on a lie, yet it took him a great deal of recovery before he recognized that he had fooled himself in thinking that he had the "perfect marriage." When they took off their rose-colored glasses, they saw each other and their relationship in a less favorable, but more realistic, light.

As you develop the ability to evaluate yourselves and your relationship as Mutual Partners honestly, you, too, will probably need to trade some of your idealism for realism. Superman may start to look a little more like Clark Kent, and Wonder Woman may suddenly seem more like her alter-ego, Diana Prince. But as you come to this honest realization, you will also understand that you are both still lovable and worth loving—with all your individual human flaws. The best relationships in recovery develop when both partners commit themselves to honesty and openness—even when doing so involves acknowledging their imperfections. By tolerating your own and each other's imperfections, you will make your relationship more real, more honest, and more human.

HOW TO KEEP COMMUNICATION OPEN AND HONEST

As you have seen, in making a commitment to work on improving your relationship with another person—whether that person is a parent, sibling, lover, spouse, or friend—you need to make honesty and openness high priorities. Without openness and honesty, people and relationships stagnate—or even regress. In striving toward Mutual Partnership, you and your partner will need to be as honest as you can in facing reality—working to eliminate denial, illusory myths, unrealistic expectations, and unrealizable ideals. And in dealing with each other, and with everyone else around you, try to be as honest as you possibly can—unless, of course, your honesty would harm others. Remember, however, that you will never be perfectly honest because, like the rest of us, you are an imperfect creature.

Although it may be impractical or unrealizable to be completely honest in some cases, by holding complete honesty "in all our affairs" as your ideal, you will give yourself and your relationships a target to aim toward. Open and honest communication does not come easily to most people, especially those who are recovering from alcoholism and codependency —illnesses that carry dishonesty and deception in their wake. But because communication is a skill, you can learn it, practice it, and improve on it throughout your life. As you try to improve your communications skills, concentrate on developing your talents to observe the following basic rules:

1. *Initiate open communication.* Don't always wait for someone else to bring up a sensitive issue. Take the initiative. The more openly and honestly you share, the more open and honest feedback you are likely to get.

2. *Listen with both ears and watch with both eyes.* Concentrate as much as you can on what the other person is saying in words. But at the same time, listen to the other person's tone of voice and watch his or her demeanor. Again, though, if you think you sense some underlying emotions or attitudes through your observation of the person's tone, body language, or demeanor, don't rely solely on guesswork or mind reading. Check out your impressions with the only one who really knows what the other person is thinking or feeling: the other person.

3. *Try to communicate openly and honestly with everyone,* not just with one particular person. You can't rely solely on one person for all your open and honest communication. Sometimes, you will need to share your feelings with a third person, especially if you have a problem with your partner. If you are open and honest with more people, you will open yourself up to more feedback and help when you need it.

4. *Think before you speak.* For the most part, you probably need to work on saying what you feel when you feel it, but try not to use your feelings as a carte blanche to attack someone else. Don't just dump all your feelings on the other person. If you phrase your words carefully and thoughtfully, your listener is more likely to hear what you are saying. Consider how the other person will respond to your words. Since words sometimes come out the wrong way in the heat of the moment, use your internal "editor"—the inner voice that questions the appropriateness and timeliness of your comments.

5. *Make "I" statements instead of "You" statements.* For example, if another person does or says something that hurts you, try to say, "I felt hurt when you . . ." instead of "You stink because you. . . ." Since "I" statements are less blaming, they allow you to say what you feel when you feel it, without making the other person feel overly defensive.

6. *Respect the other person's wish to disengage from a conversation.* You can't force people to communicate against their will. It may seem like the perfect time for you to get into a heavy discussion with someone close to you, but the other person may feel it's the wrong time. Accept and respect this feeling. If you believe this discussion is so important that it's essential to your relationship, then try to schedule a future date when you will both feel comfortable discussing it.

7. *No comment.* You don't always have to comment on what the other person says if you disagree with it. Feel free to say nothing or to say, "I hear what you're saying" or "I'm sorry you feel that way." Obviously, this doesn't mean you should sit in stony silence or withdraw in hostility because you don't like or agree with what the other person is saying. But if you feel you can react only with anger, you may be better off postponing any response.

8. *Set strict limits on permissible communication.* When words or actions become abusive, communication no longer has any meaning. No one has the license to be verbally or physically abusive to you in "trying to make a point." Remember always to give yourself permission to remove yourself from any interchange that you consider unhealthy, unproductive, or abusive. In withdrawing, simply say something like, "I find your remarks insulting and your behavior unacceptable. I can't listen to this anymore. I need to take care of myself." Don't allow communication to go beyond the limit of mutual respect.

Mastering these communications skills will simultaneously help you hear and be heard in your personal relationships. Even if you sometimes fall short of these goals, you will improve your ability to communicate by aiming toward them. As your communications skills develop, you will find it easier and easier to become more honest and open. Honest and open communication is the vehicle that carries individuals and relationships to growth and fulfillment. As your relationships become more and more intimate through your increased openness and honesty, they will mature into more equal, adult, and Mutual Partnerships.

8

CONFLICT RESOLUTION

Putting Communication to Work

As you continue to improve your communications skills as Mutual Partners, one of the biggest challenges you will need to face together will be to settle conflicts peacefully and to your mutual satisfaction. A meeting of the minds, no matter how open and honest they both may be, does not always proceed smoothly and agreeably. Since individuals have different histories, they naturally bring separate perspectives and distinctive frames of reference into their relationships. And even in the best relationships, these individual differences inevitably produce at least some degree of conflict—the day-to-day disagreements that arise whenever two people come together.

Although everyone has some conflict in his or her relationships, not all people express their conflicting feelings. While some people let the fur fly, others silently seethe, refusing even to acknowledge conflict. The actions of these people, however, tend to speak louder than their words. When two people avoid, repress, or refuse to acknowledge conflict, the tension between them builds, becoming "so thick you could cut it with a knife," as the old expression goes.

Whether you acknowledge it or not, you can't simply wish

conflict away. Most people instinctively react to conflict by thinking, "If only you loved me, you'd agree with me." But this kind of immature and wishful thinking actually tends to escalate conflict instead of resolving it. This attitude refuses to accept another person's right to differ from you, essentially sending the message, "If you really love me, you have to think, feel, and be exactly like me." But while this attitude diminishes people's right to be individuals, it augments their power. It places all responsibility for resolving disagreements—and all power to change—in the hands of the other person. Mutual Partners, however, don't resort to wishful thinking when faced with a conflict; they tackle the challenge of resolving it head-on.

THE CHALLENGE OF CONFLICT

The first step toward resolving conflict as Mutual Partners involves honestly acknowledging its existence. It may make it easier for you to admit the reality of disagreements if you recognize that conflict is essential to your individual growth, as well as to the maturation of your relationship. All real growth comes through mutual interaction. And unless you're dealing with a clone, which would neither encourage growth nor widen your perspective, every interaction inevitably involves a clash of needs, opinions, and feelings. So you can surely expect disagreements in all your relationships, but you can also be grateful for their contribution to your growth and the growth of your Mutual Partnership.

Try to look on conflict as a challenge. Through your recovery, you hope to find some serenity and balance in your life and in your relationships—qualities of life that alcoholism and codependency made impossible. But the disagreements that crop up in your day-to-day life will test your personal serenity and threaten the balance of your relationships. For this reason, you need to approach conflict as a major challenge in your recovery. The way you handle conflict and resolve disagreements can restore your peace of mind and the balance in your relationships.

Learn to anticipate conflicts with the assurance and trust that you and your partner, with the help of your higher power, can face and work them through. By working together, you two can overcome conflicts and become even more intimate. In fact, the major task in building relationships involves resolving conflicts. If you accept the risk and challenge presented by conflict, you will probably gain a heightened awareness of yourself, the other person, and your relationship.

If you recognize that conflict does *not* inevitably lead to separations or breakups, you will know that you no longer need to fear the challenge it presents. Not all differences are irreconcilable, and not all conflicts are unresolvable. Indeed, most conflicts can be resolved amicably if both people are willing to communicate and work toward that end. If you trust your mutual commitment, you will know that you don't need to be afraid to disagree with the other person and you don't need to be afraid of your partner's disagreements with you.

Mutual Partnerships work best when both people make a commitment to work on the relationship—and to work out their disagreements—together. Thus when conflicts inevitably arise, Mutual Partners need to direct their work toward reconciliation. Since conflict may initially create some distance between you, you need to approach conflict resolution with the goal of coming closer together again. Yet if both of you stubbornly get stuck trying to "force" the other person to change or trying to prove that one of you is "right" and the other is "wrong," reconciliation becomes impossible. Can you let go of the sort of black-and-white thinking that sees only right or wrong possibilities in arguments? If you learn to view conflict as a means of mutual enlightenment, rather than as an adversarial situation, you will begin to embrace conflict rather than avoid it.

Mutuality implies a certain amount of give and take in a partnership. Conflict challenges you to make this give-and-take ideal a reality. If you approach it with a constructive attitude, the given and take of compromise and negotiation will increase the intimacy you both feel. So as you tackle conflict and disagreements in your Mutual Partnership, keep the following facts about conflict in mind:

1. Conflict is normal and necessary.
2. Conflict can be resolved.
3. Conflict is not something to fear.
4. Conflict is a challenge and an opportunity.
5. Conflict can help you, the other person, and your relationship grow.
6. Conflict should involve a mutual recognition of the right to individual differences.
7. Conflict can help clarify communication.
8. Conflict can build rather than destroy relationships.
9. Conflict can promote intimacy.

If you both have committed yourself to striving toward a Mutual Partnership in your relationship in recovery, you can work things out together. In making this commitment to each other, you have already pledged yourselves to bring love, patience, tolerance, flexibility, awareness, acceptance, and understanding into your relationship. By allowing these qualities to pervade your relationship in your moments of dissension, as well as in your moments of total union, you will go a long way toward building a Mutual Partnership in deed and in name. You will find yourselves willing and able to tackle the conflicts and solve the problems that come up in the course of any relationship. And in dealing honestly with each other in conflict, you will both move toward enhanced understanding, positive change, productive resolution, and increased intimacy.

*   *   *

HOW DO YOU DEAL WITH CONFLICT?

Exploring your family history can provide important clues to how you deal with conflict. You received most of your basic training in approaching or avoiding conflict during your childhood. As a child, you learned certain ways of expressing—or not expressing—differences of opinion. You may have concluded that this was simply the way things were done. And in entering new relationships, you may have assumed that other people approached conflict in exactly the same way. A difference in approaches to conflict can, in itself, create further conflict in relationships.

Eileen, for instance, got so frustrated with her husband Ray's withdrawal from conflict that she brought it up in one of their counseling sessions. They had been trying to plan a long weekend together for weeks, but Ray kept "drifting away" whenever Eileen tried to bring the subject up. She really wanted to go skiing, but because she knew Ray hated cold weather, she wanted to make sure that he would have a good time, too. The more she tried to get Ray to admit what he wanted to do, however, the quieter and more acquiescent he became. In my office, Ray repeated a familiar refrain: "Whatever you want is fine with me."

Eileen responded, "You always say that, but I don't know when you mean it anymore. I want you to enjoy this vacation, too, and you just don't sound very enthusiastic. If you want to do something different, why don't you tell me? Are you agreeing with me just because you want to make me happy? If so, it would make me happier if you would tell me the truth. Why can't you tell me what you really feel?"

With Eileen's encouragement, Ray acknowledged that he would prefer a weekend at a beachfront resort to one at a ski resort. He couldn't say why he had felt so reluctant to level with her before, but he promised to think about it. The next week, he admitted that in most of his relationships, he tended to yield to other people's wishes to avoid a disagreement. He'd go along with almost anything rather than risk the "unpleasantness" of an argument. As a child, Ray had been the "peace-maker" in his family. Both his parents had been violent alcoholics, and they had argued constantly and ferociously to get their own way. In attempting to avoid his parents' wrath, Ray had learned early that the best strategy was to agree with all people, no matter what they said. He had gotten into the habit of keeping his opinions to himself.

Eileen helped Ray see that she wasn't like either of his parents. She explained that her family had lived by the rule: "Be as honest as you can, no matter what." She preferred Ray to tell her what he really felt, rather than reluctantly comply and then build up secret resentments. The "dishonesty" of his silent compliance frustrated her far more than the fact that he had a different opinion. Brought together by this new understanding of each other, Ray and Eileen made a commitment to express their differences of opinion honestly and then work together to *tackle* and resolve conflict, rather than avoid it.

You and your partner may find it helpful to explore how patterns of interaction in your familes may have become part of your own repertoire. Think about how your families resolved conflict. Do most members of your family tend to have emotional outbursts when faced with any conflict? Or do they opt for the "silent treatment" when differences arise? Do family members flee or fight in times of crisis? Do they avoid conflict or face it head-on? Do family fights ever get physical? Do family members tend to talk about their feelings or deny them? Do any of them attempt to avoid conflict by covering up their feelings through smoking, drinking, or overeating? Do any of your relatives refuse to see or speak to one another because of unresolved family conflicts? What patterns of handling conflict did each of you pick up in childhood? Do you still follow these patterns when confronted with conflict today?

The answers to these questions can often pinpoint areas that you and your partner or both of you may need to work on to improve your ability to resolve conflicts. Do you want to maintain or change the old familiar themes carried over from your childhood? Do you want to continue to react in ways that follow a family script that you never wrote? Or would you rather change, writing your own script for conflict resolution? You and your partner need to bring your separate approaches to conflict into harmony, so you can work together to move toward resolution. And the honest acknowledgment of conflict, as Ray discovered, is a terrific place to start.

HISTORY AS DESTINY?

In addition to providing clues to how you deal with conflict, exploring your family history can help you discover the origins of your particular differences of opinion or attitude. Indeed, you and your partner may be able to short-circuit some conflicts simply by realizing that the argument you're having today really stems from an argument that one (or both) of you had in the past. A disagreement you may have with someone else may simply involve the clash of opinions and perspectives formed by your distinctive personal histories. By discussing how the past has affected your current perceptions, you will increase each other's understanding and acceptance. And, in themselves, these qualities can resolve many conflicts.

After years of battling, Sam and Cynthia brought their most basic and persistent conflict into my office. Sam complained that Cynthia was a "slob" and that their house looked like a "disaster area"; Cynthia replied that Sam was an "obsessive neatnik," far too "picky" for her liking. Sam's attitude of "when in doubt, throw it out," went directly up against Cynthia's "you never know when you might need this." This clash of philosophies, repeated over and over again in arguments about how their house should look, created the biggest conflict in their relationship.

With my encouragement, they agreed to discuss their backgrounds during one of our sessions. Cynthia began by talking about her grandparents, who had raised their children during the depression, instilling in Cynthia's mother the idea that survival demanded extraordinary resourcefulness. Widowed at thirty-five, Cynthia's mother had raised three children on a housekeeper's income, further reinforcing the idea that scrimping and saving were the only way to survive. Cynthia's tendency to save things that might be "useful" later was thus a natural outgrowth of her background. She saved hundreds of magazines and papers because she thought that she might need to go through them again some day if she ran out of ideas for her interior-decorating career. Her childhood deprivation also made her appreciate having nice things around—like the ceramic animal figures that "cluttered up" the house, according to Sam.

Sam explained that he had been raised in a military family, the son and grandson of career naval officers. Sam's father had run a strict "tight ship" at home, demanding that both his sons keep their rooms "shipshape." Sam absorbed this attitude and carried it into his adult life. His desire to "clear the decks" demanded ordered surroundings. He wanted every surface in the house to be bare and every unused article to be out of sight.

In exploring the roots of their differences, Cynthia and Sam moved toward resolving their conflict. Although they had shared the facts of their family backgrounds before, they had never heard them presented in connection with their argument about neatness and messiness. Exploring and discussing these roots did not change either of their basic philosophies, but it did increase their understanding of each other. They accepted the fact that Sam's "cleaning up and throwing out" was just as much a part of his personality as Cynthia's "saving and collecting" was part of hers. By understanding and accepting each other's basic philosophy, they formed a solid base for compromise and negotiation.

They still disagreed about how the house should ideally look, but that was okay. At the same time, they understood that their home was, in fact, neither "too ordered" nor "too messy." Those past judgments simply reflected their different perspectives. Without changing their personalities or giving up their basic preferences, Sam and Cynthia were able to resolve their conflict by making some simple accommodations to each other. Cynthia agreed to make an effort to "confine her clutter" to her study. And Sam built bookcases to store Cynthia's magazines and papers and a display case for her ceramics.

By listening and learning about the impact of history on their present attitudes and feelings, Sam and Cynthia found a way to end this extended conflict quickly and quietly. They managed to reach a peaceful resolution through mutual understanding and accommodation. As you already know from the experience of your personal recovery, sharing, in itself, can be healing. By sharing with someone you love, you will discover that the same is true for relationships in recovery. By looking together at your families and how they did things, the two of you may gain an understanding of past influences or attitudes that tend to create ongoing conflicts in your present relationships. And this understanding will help promote negotiation and compromise toward resolution.

REACTIONS AND OVERREACTIONS

If you find yourself or someone you love overreacting to a particular conflict, it usually means that you need to explore your family histories as Sam and Cynthia did. Whenever you think that you have overreacted to something the other person has said or done, regard that overreaction as a "red flag." Stop and ask yourself where that reaction may be coming from. Sometimes it helps to step back and look at the whole map if you want to see where you are now. By looking at past circumstances, you may find an explanation of a reaction that you consider extreme, given the present circumstances.

"Lenny had been out of work for over a year and he was really depressed. Still, he was out there every single day, looking for work. It was tough, and I really admire him for it. But what really bothered me was my own reaction to the situation," confesses Sara. "I found myself getting angrier and angrier, while at the same time trying to cover up that rage. I got down on myself for not being more supportive. I wanted us to be able to face this problem together, but my anger made me really critical of him.

"The source of my anger finally came out in one of our couples sessions. As I talked about my feelings, I suddenly realized how much of that anger was left over from my childhood. My dad had never been able to hold down a 'real job' for very long, and he finally walked out on us when I was a teenager. That was the end of his financial support of our family.

"When Lenny lost his job, I got really frightened that the same thing would happen all over agian. I was afraid that he'd become a failure like my father was. And I didn't want Lenny to abandon me, too. I knew there was no real evidence that any of that would happen. But those old tapes kept going around in my head."

Sara's overreaction shows how too much old baggage can weigh you down on new journeys. Despite her rational understanding that Lenny is not the same person her father was, she associated them when Lenny lost his job. And these associations dredged up old memories, emotions, fears, and reactions. In spite of her wish to be sympathetic and supportive, the conflict created by these associative feelings made it difficult.

Overreactions often serve as important clues to unresolved family business. And unresolved conflict from the past undeniably interferes with present relationships. Dealing with the lingering effects of the past once and for all will make it easier for you to deal with the conflicts of the present. So whenever you find yourself overreacting to a current dilemma, you may find it helpful to do a little more of the Pioneering work of self-exploration. On your own, or with the help of a therapist or supportive member of a self-help group, consider similar situations from your personal history when you felt anxious, angry, or depressed. Then, share your discoveries with a Mutual Partner or someone else whom you trust. You need to find a way to expel the feelings that you bottled up so long ago.

"I'm working on my abandonment fears in individual therapy, at Al-Anon meetings, and in my relationship with Lenny," explains Sara. "My therapist suggested that I try to write a letter to my father, expressing all the feelings I had as a sixteen-year-old, when he left us. And even though I never mailed the letter, I felt better about myself after several drafts.

"What really helped the most was letting Lenny read the letter and discussing it with him. Sharing that extremely painful period of my life helped both of us see where all that irrational fear was coming from. Putting my pain in perspective and bringing my fears out in the open allowed me to let go of them. Lenny was really great about the whole thing. He told me that he understood my fears, and he reassured me that he would never abandon me the way my father did. In fact, he told me that he was afraid that *I'd* abandon *him* because he thought he was a failure. Now, knowing what I know about myself and about Lenny, I can be less reactive and more supportive about Lenny's unemployment. I know we're in this thing together."

By stepping back to do some Pioneering exploration of her unfinished family business, Sara was able to resolve her conflicting feelings and strengthen her Mutual Partnership. In honestly sharing their feelings and fears of abandonment, she and Lenny actually increased their intimacy and commitment to each other. Although the problem of Lenny's unemployment did not disappear, they did repair the dissension that had arisen out of it. They felt closer to each other than ever before and felt confident that, with each other's support, they could solve their problems together.

Just as your overreaction can alert you to the need for some additional work as a Pioneer, your Mutual Partner's overreaction can serve as a red flag, too. Whenever you feel that someone you love has overreacted to some conflict in your relationship, try to overcome your instinctive reaction of taking it personally. Do your best to detach from the overreaction, recognizing that it comes from someplace other than his or her interaction with you. Tell yourself that your partner meant to deliver that message to someone else, at another time and place. And since it wasn't really meant for you, you don't need to accept it.

At the same time, however, try to avoid automatically dismissing another person's "overreaction." Denial can be a tricky and powerful force, encouraging us to dismiss any remark that touches on some sore point or a fact about ourselves that we'd rather not acknowledge. Be careful not to label every critical remark an "overreaction" just because you'd rather not hear it. Try to evaluate another person's "overreaction" calmly and objectively before you contest, dismiss, or deny it.

To give yourself time to assess it and to avoid fueling the other person's fire, don't immediately rush in to set the record straight when you think the alcoholic has overreacted. If you still feel the other person overreacted after things have settled down a bit, you may choose a calm moment to ask where that powerful emotional reaction may have come from. Encourage the other person to explore the overreaction. By examining the past, your partner may find the source of his or her profound rage or sorrow. Remember, however, that though you can sometimes make helpful suggestions, you cannot force anyone else to undergo a Pioneering journey of self-exploration, nor can you control the course of that journey. Even when you have some clues about the roots of another person's overreaction, you cannot make the other person see those connections the same way you see them. In encouraging someone else to take a Fourth-Step "inventory," be careful to avoid taking that person's inventory yourself.

Remember, however, that it isn't taking someone else's inventory to stand up for yourself. If your partner's overreaction is in the form of physical or verbal abuse, you have every right to call it a foul shot. Remove yourself physically if that's the only way out, but, in any case, let the other person know that you won't put up with any kind of abuse. The line between overreaction and abusive behavior is sometimes a thin one, but when anyone slips over that line and becomes threatening, don't sit still for it. Regardless of where this sort of overreaction really comes from, it is totally unacceptable behavior. No one has a right to escalate conflict into abuse.

DEALING WITH DIFFERENCES

Once you have acknowledged the existence of conflicts in your relationships and explored as best you can the possible source of some of these conflicts, you can move toward resolving them. Although conflict can be resolved in a number of ways, resolution most often comes through one of the following: (1) situational change, (2) accommodation, (3) no change—mutual respect, (4) individual change, or (5) negotiation and compromise.

1. *Situational Change.* The situation that prompted the disagreement in the first place changes, resolving the conflict by removing it. Since the outcome of the conflict no longer matters, there's little point in continuing to argue. In most cases, situational change is out of the control of either person involved in the conflict.

2. *Accommodation.* One person gives in, goes along, or comes around to the other person's perspective. Sometimes, a real change in one person's point of view, arrived at through the other person's persuasive argument, may prompt this accommodation, in which case the conflict is truly resolved. But just as often, the accomodator gives up the argument as a way of avoiding or drawing a curtain over conflict. Though this kind of accommodation temporarily buries the conflict, it does not truly resolve anything. The resentments sparked by this kind of accommodation will inevitably unearth the conflict again, somewhere down the line.

Sharon and Lou, for example, had a persistent conflict in their social life. Sharon consistently wanted to leave parties earlier than Lou did. She thought it might help if they could mutually set a specific time to leave parties, so that she would get home at a "reasonable hour," but Lou always wanted to "hang loose." She tried discussing it with him several times, but each time he quickly dismissed the subject by assuring her that next time would be different. Yet even when she took the trouble to remind him before the next party, the conflict would come up again by the end of the evening. In the end, Sharon always gave in, waiting until Lou was ready to leave the party. Yet this accommodation left her feeling powerless, frustrated, and extremely angry. The conflict had not gone away; it was still simmering, just below the surface.

3. *No Change—Mutual Respect.* Resolution does *not* always mean agreement. No matter how hard you each try to convince the other to embrace your point of view, not all disagreements can be settled. But you don't have to end a disagreement to end the conflict between you. When both of you stick to your guns and refuse to change under any circumstances, the only possible resolution involves mutually coming to respect each other's right to differ. When you love another person—a spouse, a parent, a sibling, an adult child, a friend, or any other person—and have formed an emotional commitment to each other as Mutual Partners, part of that commitment should involve agreeing to disagree.

Of course, agreeing to disagree doesn't mean that you can't try to get the other person to see things your way. But you need to accept that even after hearing your case, the other person may still disagree with you—and this doesn't mean that he or she is stupid, crazy, or in any way inferior. The Serenity Prayer may help reinforce your acceptance of the other person's disagreement ("things you cannot change"). Cynthia and Sam resolved their conflict about the amount of "clutter" in their house by accepting each other's essential differences. They recognized that even though they couldn't change their opposing philosophies to come to an agreement, they could respect each other's differences and show some consideration for each other's feelings and opinions. In the sense that neither person changes his or her basic position, no change—mutual respect is a passive way to resolve conflict. But though the disagreement itself doesn't disappear, the conflict does.

4. *Individual Change.* When your partner refuses to change under any circumstances, you may need to take the initiative to alter the situation or to change yourself in a way that will resolve the conflict. Often, the action you take in changing will eventually induce your partner to change, too.

Recently, after yet another late night at a party, Sharon came to the realization that she could not force Lou to compromise. Knowing that Lou's approach was to ignore the conflict, pretending it didn't exist, she recognized that any change would have to come from her. So she stopped to consider her options:

a. She could go to parties with Lou and continue to implore him to leave when she wanted to go (maintaining the status quo).

b. She could stop going to parties with Lou altogether (situational change).

c. She could stop pleading and resign herself to staying at parties long after she wanted to leave, a situation that would make her feel miserable and resentful (accommodation).

d. She could stop accommodating and feeling like a victim and come up with an alternative action that would demonstrate that she had some power in this situation (individual change).

By listing her options in this way, Sharon could clearly see that the first three alternatives would only increase her resentments and widen the gulf between her and Lou. So she decided that rather than wait endlessly for Lou to compromise, she would take the initiative to change herself and the situation in a way that might resolve the conflict to their mutual satisfaction. She decided to come up with a plan that could satisfy both their needs and desires, even though it might not settle their difference of opinion about *when* to leave.

"I decided to bring up the party issue on a Sunday afternoon because I knew Lou would be in a relaxed, good mood after watching some sports on TV," Sharon explains. "I started by saying that neither one of us was probably happy with our repeated arguments about when to leave parties. I told him that I really could understand his wanting to stay out late, but that for me, it was just impossible. I mean, I love parties, too, but when I know that our two preschoolers will have me up at dawn, I also want to be well rested. Since I work full time and try to do household chores on Saturdays, Sundays are really important for me and the kids. I feel I owe them a calm, rested mom instead of an overtired, angry mom. And that means I have to get a good night's sleep on Saturdays, party or no party.

"After explaining my side of the conflict, I laid out my proposal. I suggested that the next time we went out, we should decide beforehand when we would leave for home—not down to the minute or anything, but setting up a clear target that we could aim for. I explained that this sort of 'flexible deadline' would make me much more comfortable than just waiting and wondering.

"But I added that I couldn't just leave it at that any longer. So I told him that if he wasn't ready within an hour of that 'deadline,' I was going to put 'Plan B' into action. I would politely excuse myself, tell the hostess I had to get home, and let Lou know I was leaving. Then I'd call a cab and make my exit as inconspicuously as possible, so that it wouldn't embarrass either one of us.

"As I outlined my plan, I tried to be as clear and calm as I could. I tried to make him see that I wasn't threatening him, but I needed to take care of myself and my needs, and I had let things slide too often in the past. This time, I had the definite feeling that Lou heard me. He seemed to know that I was going to follow through with Plan B if I had to."

Whenever you find yourself in a conflict that demands some sort of active resolution and your partner ignores the conflict and refuses to change, you might do well to follow Sharon's example of reaching an individual-change resolution. First, clearly identify the conflict and acknowledge the other person's right to opinions and needs that are different from yours. But recognize your right to fulfill your needs, just as much as your partner's right to meet his or her own. See if you can come up with a compromise plan that may fulfill both of your needs.

The, lay your plan out to your partner, presenting it in an unthreatening manner. Try to pick a time when you both feel comfortable. Start by verbally acknowledging the reality of conflict. Bring it out into the open and share your feelings about it. Explain your needs, being careful not to imply that your needs are any more important than your partner's. Offer your own two-part plan. With the first half, try to suggest some sort of mutually satisfying compromise. But with the second half, the back-up plan to use just in case the compromise plan doesn't work, draw your own bottom line. State clearly and confidently what you will do to ensure that your needs are met, too. Finally, make sure you give your Mutual Partner the opportunity to express his or her feelings.

"I have to admit I was surprised by all this," Lou acknowledges. "At first I thought she was making a big deal out of nothing. But when she explained about the kids, I could see her point of view. Sharon and I don't go to that many parties, so when we do, I always want to have a really good time. I admit I tend to get a little carried away with the moment. But when I'm having a good time at a party, it's hard for me to think about what's going to happen the next day.

"Next time, I'll try to be more aware of her needs and stick to our agreement. But I know I've made that promise before and I can understand why she might think I'll pull the same old trick again. So even though Sharon's Plan B sounds unnecessary to me, I guess she has a right to it. The way she presented it to me, I can't think of any argument against it. She didn't blame me, she didn't get hysterical, and she didn't begrudge me my fun. She just sounded like she wanted to take care of herself, and who can argue with that?"

In taking the initiative to change in this way, as Sharon

discovered, you may actually encourage your partner to change. Through her reasonable presentation, she got Lou to acknowledge the reality of the conflict in a way he never had before. Together, they agreed to aim for the compromise plan, with the understanding that the bottom-line plan was ready in the wings if needed. By coming up with a plan of your own, presenting it to the other person, and allowing a response, as Sharon did, you may be able to move toward the "ideal" resolution of conflict in a Mutual Partnership: mutual negotiation and compromise.

5. *Negotiation and Compromise.* The ideal resolution of conflict, because it demands mutual give-and-take, involves recognizing the problem together and working as a team to come up with a solution through discussion, negotiation, and compromise. Negotiation and compromise bring together the three Cs of Mutual Partnership: *commitment,* dedication to *common goals,* and *communication.* You have to make sure you communicate your own needs clearly and try to understand and accept your partner's different needs. But this honest communication only provides a starting point for negotiation and compromise. Bound by mutual commitment, you both need to agree to do what you can to change yourselves, the situation, or both if you want to achieve the common goal of reconciliation.

Does all this sound simple? Don't fool yourself; of course, it isn't. Negotiation and compromise will put your improving communications skills to the acid test. To facilitate negotiation and compromise, both of you will need to agree to talk honestly about your own needs, opinions, and feelings and listen carefully to each other's expression of those needs, opinions, and feelings. In addition to testing your communications skills, negotiation and compromise simultaneously gauge your mutual commitment and willingness to work toward common goals. Each of you will need to take action and change willingly to fulfill your mutual needs, while respecting each other's opinions and considering each other's feelings. For all these reasons, negotiation and compromise are extremely difficult. Yet by meeting these challenges together, you will strengthen your Mutual Partnership.

Your mutual willingness to negotiate and compromise will make it easier for you to tackle conflict together, rather than avoid or ignore it. As you try to move toward a peaceful resolution of your conflict, keep the following general guidelines for negotiation and compromise in mind:

a. Be mutually aware that a conflict exists.

b. Think about what you see, hear, want, and feel in regard to this conflict.

c. Share these impressions with your partner.

d. Ask your partner to share what he or she sees, hears, wants, and feels in regard to this conflict.

e. Listen carefully.

f. Identify and discuss what each of you hopes to accomplish in addressing this problem together. Set goals and establish priorities together that you hope to achieve in resolving this difficulty.

g. Take responsibility, both individually and as a team, to come up with some options or actions that may resolve the conflict to your mutual satisfaction, in a way that will achieve your goals and your highest priorities.

h. Discuss the pros and cons of each option with each other. Engage in a little flexible give-and-take if necessary. Be willing to sacrifice some of your lower priorities to meet your partner's high priorities, and vice versa.

i. Agree on a mutually acceptable course of action to implement change. Each of you needs to make an equal effort in your commitment to follow this plan together.

j. After putting your plan into action, follow up on it. Continue to discuss it with each other, deciding together what has worked and what hasn't. If either of you is still unsatisfied with the way things have worked out so far, try other options, repeating the process of negotiation and compromise until you arrive at a true resolution, one that satisfies most of your individual and relationship needs and priorities.

If you consistently follow these guidelines for negotiation and compromise, applying your improving communications skills to the thorny task of resolving differences, you will feel secure in your ability to tackle any problems that come up in your relationship as Mutual Partners. You will no longer need to come up with unilateral decisions that you impose on the other person. Instead, you will know that you can reach decisions and resolve conflict together, in a way that involves each of you taking equal responsibility to improve your relationship in recovery.

You may think that the conflicts resolved by the Mutual Partners in this chapter were not so earth shattering. To you, they may have seemed like much ado about nothing. But to an outsider, the difficulties that crop up in your own relationships may seem just as mundane. Yet it is these small-scale conflicts and tiny disagreements that most often create the trouble and unpleasantness in ongoing relationships. For this reason, the way we handle them provides one of the best measures of a relationship's strength. If you can learn to resolve these day-to-day conflicts peacefully, you will go a long way toward ensuring that your relationships in recovery will blossom into truly Mutual Partnerships.

9

FIGHTING FAIR

When Conflict Escalates

When Mutual Partners find themselves unable to resolve a
conflict, the conflict often escalates into a full-fledged fight—
not a knock-down, drag-out physical altercation, but a verbal,
and often highly emotional, exchange. The difference between
conflicts and fights is mostly a matter of degree. Whenever
conflict lingers without resolution for an excessive amount of
time, the combatants tend to become entrenched, and the level
of emotions, whether expressed or unexpressed, tends to rise
dramatically. This addition of a high degree of emotion is what
differentiates conflicts from fights. And with all that additional
emotion, people sometimes risk saying things they don't really
mean. To avoid this danger, you will need to observe new rules
designed to ensure "fair fighting."

The existence of fighting, like conflict itself, does not necessarily mean that your relationship is in trouble. Indeed, a good,
fair fight can help you avoid more serious troubles. Unfortunately, not all fights are good or fair. Some fights create far
more trouble in a relationship than they solve. And the attitude
of the combatants plays the biggest part in determining
whether the outcome of a fight will be productive or destructive.

A "bad" or unfair fighter

- is disrespectful;
- doesn't validate differences;
- engages in character assassination;
- is verbally or physically abusive;
- reads minds inaccurately and then attacks based on those wrong readings;
- refuses to change, demanding that the other person change instead;
- shirks responsibility by making excuses and rationalizations;
- blames or lays guilt trips on the other fighter;
- increases the other fighter's defensiveness;
- ends up locking both fighters into stubborn stances;
- tramples relationships.

In contrast, the "good" or fair fighter

- respects different views and feelings;
- feels free to express angry or hurt feelings, though not in a hurtful way, and encourages the other fighter to feel the same;
- doesn't let anger, fear, and hurt get out of hand;
- concentrates on the specific issue involved in the fight;
- moves toward mutual understanding;
- willingly tries to end fights, when possible, through a process of mutual accommodation and compromise;
- wants the fight to end with some reconciliation;
- nurtures relationships, even through fighting, and makes them stronger.

The attitude and approach of the fighters determines whether a fight will be productive or destructive to a relationship. As long as it doesn't deteriorate into abusiveness, fighting is inherently neither right nor wrong. Abuse, however, never solves anything; it only perpetuates more abuse. So even if you forget all the rest of the rules of fair fighting, always remember to observe the first and most important rule: *No physical violence allowed!* No hitting, smacking, shoving, pulling, beating, or biting. No physical violence—ever.

Every pair of Mutual Partners develops their own particular style of fighting. Some relationships have almost no fighting, while other relationships, although just as great, involve constant combat. Some battle it out with reason alone, while others have furious, highly charged fights. But no matter what their individual approaches to battle may be, the best relationships use their fights as a way of solving relationship problems. As long as Mutual Partners manage to keep their self-esteem intact and arrive at some sort of solution, it doesn't really matter how they get there.

Fair fighting is the attempt to settle large and lingering arguments without violence, either physical or verbal. Fair fighting recognizes that the best fights involve a meeting of equals. It takes two to tangle and two to untangle. To ensure that your fights stay fair, that they maintain equality, and that they don't deteriorate into physical or verbal violence, you'll need to observe certain ground rules. Sit down with your Mutual Partner and make a commitment to observe the following ground rules in your fights:

1. *No physical violence allowed!* This rule cannot be repeated too often. While fights can often help you strengthen your relationship, abuse *always* destroys relationships.

2. *Try to keep your voice down.* If you start to yell, your partner will probably react to your loudness instead of responding to your words. *What* you are saying gets lost in *how* you are saying it.

3. *Say what you feel when you feel it.* Make a commitment to share your emotions honestly, even when they are at their most intense level. Don't forget that this commitment means sharing the good feelings, too, not just the bad ones.

4. *Don't say it if you don't mean it.* Choose your words as carefully as you can in the heat of the moment. Although you

can apologize later or say you didn't mean it, you can never truly take your words back once they've slipped out of your mouth.

5. *Don't hit below the belt.* The better you know someone, the better you know his or her most vulnerable spots. Avoid the temptation to aim for those vulnerable spots during a fight.

6. *Don't blame, attack, or criticize your partner.* Concentrate on communicating how *you* feel by making "I" statements.

7. *Stick to the here and now.* Don't bring up old issues, third parties who aren't really involved, or any other extraneous material.

8. *Be specific.* Don't generalize or use expressions like "You never . . . " or "You always. . . . "

9. *Give each other "equal time."* Again, this means both speaking your own mind *and* listening to your partner.

10. *Don't interrupt when your partner is speaking.* Give the other person a fair chance to express feelings and opinions.

11. *Listen without becoming defensive.* Listening will be easier for the two of you if you both observe all the other rules. But even if your partner slips, don't fall into the trap of launching a counteroffensive. Just point out that your partner's words were unfair, without getting too defensive about what was said.

12. *Make a commitment to end fights peacefully.* Agree beforehand that your fight should come to some kind of peaceful ending. Don't let fights become open ended or ongoing. Even if it means agreeing on nothing more than that it's okay for you to disagree, find a way to end the fight. If you can't even agree to disagree, then call a truce or time-out and reschedule the fight for another time.

If you want, you and your partner can add your own rules to these, as long as you both agree to try your best to abide by them. As imperfect creatures, you will probably slip once in a while and break one of these ground rules. Whenever you do, apologize to your partner as soon as possible and reaffirm your commitment to "play by the rules" of fair fighting. If you do, you will begin to reap the rewards of fair fighting. *Fair* fights do the following:

1. Increase your awareness of yourself, your partner, your relationship, and your situation.
2. Encourage a two-way transmission of immediate, straightforward, and earnest messages.
3. Allow each of you to express your individual perceptions, opinions, thoughts, feelings, and needs.
4. Facilitate changes in behavior and attitude.
5. Expose fears, feelings, and vulnerabilities and promote intimacy.
6. Make both fighters feel relieved that they have survived an emotional storm and better prepared to handle the next storm.

THE NO FAULT/NO BLAME RULE

As a Pioneer, you came to realize that both self-blame and blaming others could only stand in the way of your personal growth and self-improvement. By the same token, blaming and faultfinding block the recovery of relationships as well. When you get into a fight with anyone, try to apply the no fault/no blame principle of fair fighting. Since blaming and faultfinding are in themselves attacks, they increase hostilities and make it impossible to settle a fight. In fact, they usually make other people dig their heels in even deeper. Since they entrench people in their opposing positions, blaming and faultfinding make mutuality or teamwork impossible. To make things worse, words spoken in blaming and faultfinding often pop up again somewhere down the line, causing even more fights. Eliminating blame can thus prevent or defuse many potentially damaging fights.

If you want to eliminate blame from your Mutual Partnership, you will need to understand where blame usually comes from. In human relationships, we most often heap blame on another person—or on ourselves—for "failing" to meet our expectations. We all enter relationships with certain needs and expectations. We expect ourselves to live up to one set of standards; our parents, another; our friends, a third; spouses, a fourth; and so on. In some cases, we set standards so high that no one could meet them. And so we blame ourselves or others for "failing" to live up to these unrealizable ideals. By lowering our expectations to a more realistic level, we will become less critical of ourselves and others.

Having more realistic expectations, however, does not always solve the problem of blaming and faultfinding that interferes with our movement toward Mutual Partnerships. All too often, although the people we love would like to do what they can to meet our expectations, they don't even know what we want and need from them. You may not always convey your expectations—what you want and need from your relationship—clearly. Do you sometimes think other people should know what you need without having to ask for it? If you do, then you're still falling into the trap of mind reading instead of communicating.

Some Mutual Partners find it helpful to list the ways in which their needs would be met in a "perfect" relationship. By examining your list of needs, you can get a better sense of how realistic they are. Then, exchange your list of needs with your Mutual Partner. Instead of continuing to blame your mate— or your sister or your father—state your needs through this list. Or if you've already done so, why not try to restate them in this new way, rather than blame the other person for not listening? By talking about your respective needs, you can negotiate. You can find out whether your partner thinks she or he can meet some of those needs and you can consider your partner's needs, seeing how many of them you can meet.

If you or your partner has a strong tendency to find fault with or blame others, you may need to do more than create and share your lists of what you need from the relationship. One of the best ways to counteract blame is to make a "gratitude list." Document the good things that people have done for you or continue to do for you—especially those people with whom you find fault most often. For example, if you blame your sister for forgetting your birthday or your boyfriend for always being late, write down the things they have given you in the past or the good qualities that they bring to your life today. By writing down the things you are grateful for, you will have a concrete reminder that just as none of us is perfectly good, none of us is totally awful. And remember to share this list with the other person, too. It will help you both feel good about yourselves and in so doing, it may smooth out a lingering fight.

Sharing these two lists with each other can provide you with a good starting point to get rid of some of the blame that sparks fights or adds fuel to them. These exercises will help you start to ask for what you want, give what you can give, and be grateful for what you get. If you can add these three ingredients to your relationship, you will no longer have any grounds for blaming each other.

Ultimately, mutual forgiveness is the only force that can make blame disappear in a relationship. And if you work at it together, you can nurture forgiveness in your Mutual Partnership. So if you do someone wrong, do your best to make amends so you can forgive yourself. And if someone tries to make amends for a wrong done to you, do your best to accept those amends. If you can, try to forgive your partner and recognize his or her efforts to patch things up. You will discover that if you can let go of the wrong that someone has done you, instead of holding on to it with blame, it will go away. If you work together with your Mutual Partner to eliminate blame from your relationship in recovery, then faultfinding is much less likely to prolong your fights. Once you eliminate blame, neither of you will feel inferior. You can therefore resume your fights on fairer, more equal, terms.

TIME-OUTS AND TRUCES

At any point in a fight, you or your partner should feel free to call a time-out. At times, it is necessary to put a fight on hold until a later date. You may have hit a stalemate, when the fighting seems to keep going around in circles instead of moving forward. Emotions may have gotten too far out of control, making it impossible for reason to prevail. Caught up in the fight, either or both of you may be repeatedly breaking the rules of fair fighting. For any of these reasons, or for reasons of your own, you may find it productive to call a time-out. Try to use a time-out only as a stopgap measure, when a fight becomes too heated or an apparently insurmountable impasse arises. To make sure you aren't using a time-out as a permanent avoidance strategy, if you ask for the break, you should always specify a time when you can resume the fight and continue to resolve the conflict.

Charles and Shirley reached the point when they needed a time-out in a recent fight. Charles had been critical of several episodes of Shirley's "irresponsibility" in the weeks leading up to the fight. Shirley had said little in response, allowing the tension to build up over those weeks until she finally exploded, telling Charles that she was tired of his lecturing and tired of being treated like a child. Charles claimed that her childish behavior made him treat her like a child. Angry words flew back and forth, until finally Shirley became hysterical and locked herself in the bathroom.

After calming down a bit, Shirley used this impromptu time-out to think about the fight they had just had. Much to her chagrin, she realized that she had just repeated a pattern from her childhood. Whenever her brothers or sisters had teased her, she had always ended up sobbing and running to the bathroom, where she would hide out and have a good cry. Since she didn't like to see history repeat itself in this way, she decided to calm down and think about how she might break this old pattern in her fights.

After drying her eyes, Shirley went out to the living room,

where Charles was sulking—*his* old pattern whenever a fight ended without him getting his way. "Charles," she said calmly, "I'm sorry I ran out on you, but this break is actually doing me some good. I've got a lot of things to think about, though, and I'm still too upset to discuss it right now. I just don't think we'll get anywhere if we start fighting again. How about if we agree to continue this time-out until tomorrow morning? Let's talk about it over breakfast, when we've both had a chance to cool off a little. Okay?"

When Charles agreed, they left the fight behind them and spent the evening with friends. By the next morning, they had both thought a lot about their fight. Shirley wasn't happy that she had once again acted like a wounded victim, and Charles wasn't pleased that he had resorted to name-calling and sulking. Both felt emotionally drained by the fight and had no desire to start battling again. They both apologized to each other and said that they loved each other. In making up, they both agreed to try to change for the better. In the future, Charles promised, he would try to express himself without resorting to name-calling and belittling. And Shirley promised to try not to take critical comments so personally and to ask for time-outs before she had reached the point of hysterics.

Obviously, it's hard to conceive of asking for a time-out and then following through with it when you are in the heat of a passionate fight. But if you teach yourselves to adopt the time-out rule whenever you need it, you can buy yourselves the time you may need to keep a limited fight from turning into an all-out war. In calling a time-out, you may prevent yourselves from saying a lot of things in anger that you will later regret. In Charles's and Shirley's case, even though the time-out began with hysterics, it de-escalated the fight to such an extent that neither of them felt it was necessary to continue it.

Time-outs will give you both the chance to reconsider not only your side of a fight, but your approach to the fight. If you and your partner have agreed to a time-out, try to take advantage of it. Don't envision the time-out as a chance to sharpen your claws or plot retaliation or revenge. Instead, use it productively, taking advantage of the opportunity to reflect on the fight. The big mess that had you so worked up in the middle of a fight may seem inconsequential when considered in the calmer moments of a time-out.

If you can't think about the fight without stirring yourself up again, then set it aside. Think about more pleasant things or do something unrelated to the fight. Some Mutual Partners physically distance themselves during a time-out. One of you may want to take the dog for a walk while the other takes a long, hot shower. Or, as Shirley and Charles did, you may want to do something together that will take your mind off the fight. Two of my patients in couples therapy use their time-outs to take half-hour walks with each other, when they can talk about anything *but* the fight; they put the fight on the back burner until they can approach it more calmly. Before you need to put it in effect, consider what you and your Mutual Partner would like to do during the time-out.

Remember that time-outs require time-ins, too. Although Charles and Shirley decided to wait until the next morning, some Mutual Partners try to observe the old rule, "Always make up before you go to bed." If you can do it, this rule can help ensure that fights do not fester for too long. But don't force yourself to observe this rule if it's not for you. Come up with a rule that suits both of your individual needs.

When you come together again, have the courage to apologize if you regret something you said or did during the fight. Sometimes, it can be just as important to say the two little words, "I'm sorry," as it is to say the three little words, "I love you." Unfortunately, false pride sometimes gets in the way, preventing us from admitting our mistakes or character defects. If you both teach yourselves humbly to say you're sorry when you feel you have done something wrong, you will end a lot of fights before they get out of hand. Keep in mind, however, that sometimes even apologizing is not enough to end a fight. In some cases, you will have to make a greater effort to make amends—by changing the things in yourself that you felt sorry for.

Sometimes, even after a time-out, fights cannot be settled through negotiation or compromise, and neither of you may be ready to concede or accommodate yourself to the other's position. In cases like these, you both need to recognize and accept that neither of you is ready, willing, or able to change your mind, position, attitude, or behavior. Remind yourself that a deadlock is not the worst thing in the world. If you both feel strongly about a particular issue, maybe you *shouldn't* compromise yourself or your principles in that regard. Maybe you're both right—from your own points of view—but perhaps you cannot see the dispute that objectively while you're still in the middle of it.

Unless you want a dispute like this to cast a shadow over your relationship for months or even years, you may find it worthwhile to call a truce. In a truce, you both need to acknowledge that you have different positions, but agree to give up the power play about who is "right" and who is "wrong." You agree to disagree and not bring the discussion up for a while. In this sense, a truce is like an extended time-out.

Hank and Leslie, two of my patients, had been locked in a fight for weeks. Their son Johnny had mentioned that he wanted a dog. Convinced that "every boy should have a dog," Hank thought it was a great idea. But Leslie fought against it, arguing that she already had her hands full with a three-year old and that she didn't need the "added burden" of taking care of a dog. Despite weeks of mutual pleading and dozens of reasons on each side, they couldn't settle the fight. They decided to call a truce for three months, until Johnny's birthday, before discussing the issue again. By that time, Johnny wanted a tricycle instead of a dog.

In the rare cases when you just can't settle a fight, you may want to draw up a truce with your Mutual Partner. While you are observing the truce, the situation may change, as it did for Leslie and Hank, in a way that takes care of the dispute. Or if you call a truce today, you may not even remember what you were fighting about when the truce is over. Declaring a truce and calling a mutual end to hostilities gives things a chance to settle themselves. Through your individual growth or through a change in circumstances, you may see the dispute differently when you return to it months later.

Naturally, a truce will not lead to a resolution of all fights as easily as it settled Leslie's and Hank's argument. Fights about fundamental issues, such as having children, buying a house, changing jobs, or moving to a new city, will not disappear just because you agreed to a temporary truce. The break from fighting, however, may provide each of you with an opportunity to reconsider—and perhaps change—your position in the dispute. Sometimes, even after observing a brief truce, you will still be unable to resolve a fight that involves an issue that is critical to the future of your relationship. In this kind of situation, you will probably find it helpful to consult a couples counselor or a family therapist. An impartial professional, skilled at mediating disputes, can sometimes urge two people to move toward negotiation and compromise. And this friendly push in the right direction often results in a settlement of differences.

IRRECONCILABLE DIFFERENCES

It would be lovely to think that Mutual Partners could work out all their differences. Despite our ideals about relationships in recovery, sometimes differences become irreconcilable and relationships end. Mutual Partnerships do break up: Parents and children stop speaking, siblings choose not to contact one another, married couples divorce, friends agree to stop seeing each other. Whenever two people cannot seem to resolve their disagreements—about values, belief systems, lifestyles, habits, levels of commitment, other friends, outside interests, or anything else that matters deeply to them—through goodwill, mediation, negotiation, compromise, or fighting, they have run into irreconcilable differences. These differences often become so extreme and so sensitive that they preclude any kind of meaningful relationship.

"When Russ got sober and we both got into our recovery programs, I felt sure we would be able to salvage our marriage," remembers Jerri, who, despite all her work and her husband's efforts to try to improve their twelve-year marriage, eventually divorced. "We really had high hopes. But as the months wore on, it became more and more obvious that things were not really working. The trouble had started long before recovery, and I think our history of negativity had just gone on for too long before we did anything about it. We had financial problems, work problems, problems with the kids, and relationship problems. And even though most of those problems got better in recovery, we still couldn't seem to make it as a couple."

We may find it painful to admit it, but reality doesn't always live up to our romantic and mythic expectations. Although we want to believe that "love is always forever," relationships do have lifetimes. In spite of all our wishes and desires, these lifetimes often end. Love sometimes fades, and even when it remains strong, unfortunately it does *not* always conquer all. Some relationships in recovery just don't work. Irreconcilable differences can lead to a breakup and separation in any relationship—not just in marriages, but also in friendships, in business partnerships, and among family members.

Few people like to talk about—or even think about—the pain of divorce, separation, or alienation among family members. Unfortunately, we do need to acknowledge the reality of separation. When a relationship consistently creates an enormous amount of pain for both people—or even for one person—it may be in the best interest of everyone involved for these two people to place strict limits on the amount of contact they have with each other. Among couples, this limiting of contact may mean separate bedrooms, or it may indicate a trial separation or divorce. Family members—parents and children or siblings—in a similarly painful relationship may find it less discomfiting if they see each other only on special "family" occasions. In cases that do not involve physical, sexual, or emotional abuse, I never advise my patients to cut themselves off permanently from other family members or to divorce. But

I also avoid recommending that they stay together. Individuals need to make these painful choices about separation for themselves.

In early recovery, you may have stayed in a relationship simply because you couldn't conceive of doing anything else. Since the relationship was—and probably still is—so important to you, you may have worked as hard as you could on the recovery of your relationship, as well as on your individual recovery. Indeed, you may have done everything you and your Mutual Partner thought you could or should do to make the relationship work. But if you continue to be dissatisfied and distraught, you may need to look at why you have stayed in the relationship for so long and whether it may serve the best interest of either or both of you to separate.

Don't rush into a decision about ending a marriage or any other relationship. Those of my patients who decided to divorce or end a relationship say that when they made their choice, they knew they were ready to take that step. Just as they had started seeking recovery and help for themselves when they had gotten "sick and tired of being sick and tired," they decided to leave a relationship when they became "dissatisfied with their dissatisfaction." Obviously, since individuals can tolerate different levels of pain or tolerate pain for different amounts of time, the choice to end a relationship becomes a deeply personal decision. Those who are close to you may tell you that they can't understand how you stay involved in a relationship that's dissatisfying or even painful to you. But no matter what anyone else thinks of your relationship, you and your Mutual Partner ultimately have to decide for yourselves whether to stay together or separate.

How will you know when a relationship is over? Ask yourself whether you have done everything possible to make the relationship work. Have you reached a point when you can accept that the relationship just won't work, in spite of your best efforts? If you haven't, then you may not be ready to end the relationship. Mutual Partnerships should be loving, respectful, affirming experiences—at least most of the time. If your relationship is not, it may be better for you to leave than to stay. Naturally, all relationships have their painful moments. But when the amount of pain involved in a relationship seems by far to outweigh the pleasure on a regular basis, you both may decide to accept the inevitability of a breakup. In the case of marriage, a breakup means separation or divorce. In other Mutual Partnerships, it may mean eliminating or severely limiting the communication and contact that has become a regular source of pain in your life.

"I guess there was too much disappointment, anger, and resentment on both sides," Jerri explains. "The bad news between us had just gone on for too long. I honestly think Russ tried to be more emotionally available to me and the kids when he got sober, but I still didn't feel it was enough. He still wasn't very involved with us.

"Russ was in denial about our relationship for years. He always thought it was 'fine,' but I thought it was terrible. Just one example: Russ wanted to believe our sex life was great. He insisted that sex was 'no problem' when we started to see a marriage counselor. But when I tried to discuss sex with him in therapy, when I told him that I hadn't enjoyed sex for a long time and admitted that I had been merely going along with it, Russ got very upset. He stormed out of our counselor's office and then stopped going to sessions altogether. To him, it was like I'd broken all the rules by talking about our sex life with someone else.

"I kept going to individual therapy on my own, and Russ really resented it. He wanted me to drop therapy and go to Al-Anon exclusively. That really made me angry, and I exploded, telling him to stop trying to control my life. But he told me he couldn't deal with my anger. I'd been angry for years, but now that I'd learned how to express it, he just didn't want to hear about it. He didn't want to hear about me, and he moved out of the house pretty soon after that.

"It was really hard for me to express my feelings, and I know I hurt him. But I felt like I was fighting for my life. I was trying to get better myself and, if possible, save the relationship. And for that, I had to be open and honest about all my feelings, including my anger. That was the most difficult part for me."

In listening to Jerri, one finds it easy to understand how their differences became irreconcilable. The serious breakdown in communication between Jerri and Russ made it impossible for them to deal with their difficulties. Russ tended to deny the existence of problems in the relationship, while Jerri started sinking into self-pity. Each tended to blame the other for the problems in their relationship. Perhaps because each had unrealistic expectations about the other, neither truly appreciated where the other was on his or her respective path to recovery. They both felt disappointed, angry, and hurt. Yet they were unable to confront and discuss their feelings together and unwilling to commit to staying in marital counseling in an attempt to resolve their relationship problems.

A breakdown in communication, like the one experienced by Russ and Jerri, is the most common factor that brings about the end of a relationship. When the emotional distance created by breakdowns in communication becomes too great, both people tend to withdraw. The emotional, intellectual, and spiritual connections—as well as the physical connection in the case of spouses or lovers—weaken, leaving the bond between the two people too loose to sustain a working relationship. Nothing stops them from becoming angrier, more unhappy, and more alienated from each other. If this situation has happened in your relationship, you may find that ending the relationship offers the best hope for each of your recoveries.

If you reach this conclusion, you may make a decision to terminate your relationship. But, of course, no one makes these decisions or follows through on them with ease. If you have invested an enormous amount of time, energy, and effort in a relationship, you will find it extremely painful to end it. Yet despite all your mutual efforts, you may still come to a painful moment of truth when you both realize that the relationship just won't work. And, like most people who choose to end a relationship, you may not find it easy to accept this truth emotionally, no matter how obvious it seems intellectually.

It may ease your acceptance if you realize that the ending of a relationship is not necessarily a disaster. Often, it ends up being much healthier to leave an unhealthy relationship than to stay in it. So even if your relationship—with your spouse or your lover, your sister or your brother, your father or your mother—has ended, it doesn't mean that *either* of you has failed. Indeed, in many cases, the ending of a relationship does not even mean an unhappy ending. If you both continue to work on your individual paths to recovery, you will keep growing. You will continue to learn about yourself, build your self-esteem, and increase your ability to relate to others openly and honestly. You may discover, as Jerri and Russ did, that sometimes it is easier to deal with each other when you limit the amount of contact between you.

"Actually things got much better between us after we separated. Even the kids said it was better," admits Jerri. "That awful tension that had been between us for years had finally disappeared. Everyone felt more relaxed.

"Russ actually sees the kids more and has a better relationship with them now than he ever had before. Naturally, I still think he's not as involved with them as he should be. But I know that's my hang-up. I have to work on controlling my need to control things, so I'm trying to stay out of Russ's relationship with our children. I know I'm still way too judgmental, but I've let go of some of my expectations. They do have some kind of relationship with him, and that's important to all of us.

"What was really hard for me was when Russ started dating. I'm not at the point where I can even consider getting romantically involved with anyone. Right now I'm busy enough working, taking care of the family, and dealing with myself in therapy and Al-Anon. I don't even think about having a romantic relationship very often. I'm not ready for anything like that."

Jerri and Russ are coping with the breakup of their relationship as well as they can. Because the end of any relationship—through separation or divorce—is difficult, many people find it hard to get on with their life after experiencing this trauma. Like Jerri, for instance, many women and men find it extremely stressful to date after the end of a marriage or romantic relationship. Individuals react differently to their sudden freedom to form new attachments and to the anxieties associated with this freedom. And though some newly divorced or separated people leap into relationships, most avoid them for a while. The breakup of family relationships—adult children from parents or brothers from sisters—can produce a similar effect, making both people wary of future friendships and attachments of any kind.

Acceptance is the key to getting on with your life. Letting go of a relationship, even after you have definitely decided to end it, is an enormous task. Like the death of someone you loved, the end of a life together as lovers, spouses, siblings, or other family members requires a period of mourning to put it behind you. You have already experienced a similar grieving process early in recovery, when you gave up the crutch of your addiction or codependency. If you reach out to them again, the same people who helped you through that earlier grieving process may offer you the sensitivity, sympathy, and support you need to get through your grief over the end of this relationship. Keep in mind that the profound grief you feel is a normal and necessary human response to loss. If you allow yourself to experience it instead of denying it or cutting it short, you can move forward toward the acceptance that will allow you to get on with your life.

It's important to try to let go of the relationship without blaming yourself or the other person for the breakup. Try to forgive, even when you can't forget. Jerri recognizes that she still has to work on forgiving. She sometimes gets stuck saying things like Russ "wasn't very involved" or Russ "was in denial." If she continues to hold on to the things she *thinks* he "should have" or "could have" done—and perhaps still can do?—to save the relationship, she will not truly accept the end of the relationship. Try not to get caught in the trap of constantly saying "your fault" or "my fault." To heal fully, you need to forgive yourself and the other person, giving up and turning over the hatred, blame, and anger that retards the healing process. That doesn't necessarily mean that you should condone everything that happened or absolve yourself or the other person of all responsibility. But it does mean that you must leave behind the feeling that you or the other person could have done anything differently to salvage the relationship. Instead of judging either of you as failures, accept the fact that each of you did the best you could at the time.

Even though you and your Mutual Partner couldn't make your relationship work to your mutual satisfaction, you probably learned a great deal in the process of trying to improve it. You each may have acquired a great deal of knowledge, experience, and personal growth. All relationships—whether we judge them in retrospect as good or bad—transform us. You are no longer the same person you were before the relationship. Even as you grew apart, you continued to grow as individuals. So though you may have severed yourself from your relationship to the other person, you still have yourself and your recovery. And you will carry them into all future relationships.

If you are ending a relationship, think about the many strengths and positive qualities you've brought to the relationship. These strengths are truly yours and can never be taken away from you. Remind yourself that you can take them to the next one as well. Think also about all the lessons you have learned in working on your relationship and your recovery— lessons that will never be unlearned. Aren't you a little bit wiser now? Recovery has almost definitely made you better prepared now to go on with the rest of your life.

In working on improving yourself and your relationship, you've developed some talents that will never desert you. You improved your interpersonal skills in ways that will help you in all your relationships. You've learned to communicate more honestly and openly, confront more, complain less, and resolve conflicts with another person. The same principles of recovery you've applied to this relationship, you can now practice in all your affairs. If you continue to work on them, your personal recovery, along with your improved communications skills and your new ability to work together with others to resolve conflict, will never leave you. And even though this particular relationship didn't work out, these talents will serve you well, allowing you to move into your current and future relationships as a Mutual Partner.

10

FOR "COUPLES" ONLY

*The Pleasure
Principles*

If you and your Mutual Partner are spouses or long-term lovers, your sexual relationship—like every other aspect of your
life together—will require recovery. The beginning of drinking
usually marks the beginning of the end of all true intimacy,
including sexual intimacy. As communication in general
breaks down, sexual communication and sexual activity break
down, too. As alcoholism progresses, loving expressions of
warmth and tenderness tend to decrease while resentments increase dramatically. For these reasons, alcoholism usually results not only in physical, mental, emotional, and spiritual
alienation, but in sexual estrangement: the loss of anything
resembling an active, mutually pleasurable sexual relationship.

IS THERE SEX IN SOBRIETY?

Even after both of you began to pursue your recovery, your
sex life may have remained in ruins. In the earliest weeks and
months of recovery, you probably didn't focus a tremendous

amount of time and energy on improving your sexual life. When simply getting and staying sane and sober take so much effort, few people can place sexuality high on their list of priorities. No wonder some people in early recovery wonder if there's any sex in sobriety. The old sexual chemistry, if it ever existed, seems like a thing of the distant past.

Fortunately, however, although the illness of alcoholism makes the loss of sexual intimacy inevitable, the rebirth of sexual intimacy usually is a natural by-product of the healing that takes place in recovery. Most often, this increase in sexual intimacy proceeds slowly and gradually, simultaneous with the long rehabilitation of relationships involved in recovery from alcoholism and codependency. You may doubt whether you confronted your sexuality in the Eye-Opener and Pioneer stages of recovery. But indirectly, perhaps without even realizing it, you have been laying the foundation for sexual intimacy all along. Your new commitment to being honest with yourself and others and the hard work of self-discovery have made you ready to tackle sexual intimacy.

Although the improvements in you and your relationship have already provided a secure foundation for the recovery of sexual intimacy, you can accomplish even more by focusing some of your energies on sexual recovery. To restore sexual balance as Mutual Partners, you will need to work together, applying all the other skills you have learned earlier in recovery to this specific arena. If you willingly commit yourselves to pour the same enthusiasm and effort into sexual intimacy that you have devoted to the rest of your relationship in recovery, you will certainly garner impressive results. And you will almost certainly have fun in the process.

The recovery of sexual intimacy will mirror the rest of relationship recovery. As a sexual Eye-Opener, you can no longer deny sexual problems that may exist in yourself or in your relationship. You will need to examine your sexual attitudes and behavior and make a commitment to change those that stand in the way of sexual intimacy. As a sexual Pioneer, you will need to go on a journey of sexual self-discovery, exploring your sexual identity, needs, and desires. You will need to nurture a philosophy of fun while valuing yourself sexually. Finally, as a sexual Mutual Partner, you will have to work on improving your sexual communication. You will need to practice expressing your sexual needs openly and honestly, listening when your partner voices needs, and applying your improved communications skills to the resolution of sexual conflicts. If you make a sexual commitment to each other and devote yourselves to the common goal of improved sexual intimacy, you will discover that sex can at last be mutually satisfying.

EXPLORING YOUR SEXUAL IDENTITIES

Every individual comes into a relationship with a "sexual core": a particular sexual orientation and specific sexual values, drawn from a complicated array of sources and influences. Beginning early in childhood, all our sexual experiences, including what society and our families told us about sex, helped shape the values, attitudes, feelings, thoughts, and behaviors that became the foundation of our sexual core.

Before you begin to explore your current sexual complexion, you may find it worthwhile to examine with your partner the entire complex that has formed your sexual histories. Alone and together, you and your partner may want to ask yourselves certain questions regarding your sexual upbringing. Just to get you started, ask yourselves (separately):

1. Where did I get my sex education? Who or what taught me the most about sex?
2. Was sex a taboo subject in my home? Could I talk about it with anyone?
3. Did I suffer from incest or any other inappropriate sexual behavior during my childhood? If so, have I sought professional care to help me deal with this trauma?

4. How were affection and love physically expressed in my family? Did my parents kiss or hug each other in front of us? Did they ever hug or kiss us?
5. How open was my family in talking about any kinds of feelings? Was it okay to say you were hurt, angry, disappointed, or unhappy?
6. How did my parents deal with childhood sexual exploration? Did they ever catch any of us "playing doctor" or masturbating? What did they do?
7. Did I receive negative messages about my body or about sex in general? Were "dirty" or "bad" words associated with sex or my body?
8. What religious beliefs pertaining to sexual behavior did my family share? Do I share these beliefs?
9. Did my friends and I joke or boast about sex as teenagers? What sort of things did we say?

Take plenty of time to think about these questions in depth before writing your answers. After exploring your sexual history alone, exchange your answers with your Mutual Partner and discuss them. Since these questions may open doors that have been closed for years, you may be surprised at each other's responses—and your responses as well. You may also want to consider how you present feelings about sexuality and sexual behavior conform to or vary from what you learned in your childhood. However you choose to follow up this exercise, don't stop at merely answering the questions. Share your feelings about your sexual history and about your partner's. As you exchange these intimate feelings, experiences, and reactions, the sharing will undoubtedly help you feel closer to each other than you have felt before. And this feeling, in itself, will increase your sexual intimacy.

Discussing the formation of your individual sexual values and attitudes will also help you understand the origins of most sexual conflict in your Mutual Partnership. You and your partner may have different values and expectations about when, where, and how to express your sexuality. When your sexual values clash with your partner's, you will inevitably experience some sexual conflict. To resolve this present sexual conflict, though, you may need to look to the past. Examining your sexual histories together will give you the opportunity to reconsider the definition of appropriate sexuality and sexual expression for you, for your partner, and for the two of you together. You may decide that you both need to make some sexual adjustments, fine-tuning each other's sexual values so you can move toward mutually fulfilling sexual experiences.

In reexamining your sexual values, you may begin to wonder what normal sexual behavior is. Couples who come to me with sexual problems often have a wide array of questions that pop up in the course of counseling sessions. They wonder, as you may:

Is it normal

- to have sexual intercourse every day?
- to have sexual intercourse once a month?
- to have sex when you don't feel like it?
- to expect foreplay before sexual intercourse?
- to have oral-genital sex?
- for one person to have total responsibility for birth control?
- to use "marital aids" or "erotica" in making love?
- for the same person to play the aggressive role every time?

In sexuality, as in all other areas of life, the concept of normality does not really advance a discussion. It just doesn't make sense to compare your sex life—or your recovery, or your income, or any other part of your life—with other people's. Neither statistics that offer national averages nor other individual's stories of their sexual experiences will enhance your sex life with your Mutual Partner. As two consenting and willing adults, you both need to decide for yourselves what brings you pleasure in a sexual relationship. What's normal for you may not be normal for another couple. Except for obviously deviant and criminal behavior—incest, rape, and other sexual violence—any sexual activity that you find enjoyable and that hurts neither of you nor your relationship can fall within your unique range of "normal" sexual behavior.

Since there's really no such thing as "normal" sexuality that holds true for everyone, don't worry yourselves with questions like, "Is this normal?" Instead, ask yourselves, "Do both of us enjoy what we are doing sexually? Does it mutually satisfy me and my partner? Do elements of our sex life neither harm nor destroy our relationship or ourselves in any way? Does our sex life bring us closer together?" If you can answer yes to these questions, then stop worrying about normal behavior and concentrate on your own, mutually enjoyable, sexual activity.

WHAT IS GOOD SEX?

Sex means a lot of different things to different people. Some people think of sex purely in terms of casual sex: just plain fun for its own sake, sex stripped of any other interpersonal connotations. Other people cannot conceive of sex apart from profoundly meaningful relationships. Some people use sex as a kind of drug or mood changer, while others use it as a means of expressing deep love and commitment. Sex can be all these things, and a single sexual encounter may bring many of these disparate tones together in harmony. Indeed, sex has different meanings not just for separate individuals, but for the same person at different times of her or his life. Like every other part of your life, your sex life is dynamic, constantly undergoing change. During the course of a lifetime—or the span of a relationship—our sexual attitudes and behaviors change. Even with the same partner, each new sexual interchange may take on a different shading. From day to day, you may experience sex as delightful or dull, good or bad, clean or dirty, spontaneous or planned, intimate or distanced, a joy or a duty, pleasure seeking or baby making. For most people, sex usually falls somewhere in the middle of these various extremes.

Despite these various shadings and interpretations, however, good sex should usually be mutually pleasurable. Naturally, sex may not provide the same degree of pleasurability for both partners every time. But even when it falls a little short of being a superspectacular, fireworks-exploding, all-consuming, passionate experience, you should both take some pleasure in most of your sexual intercourse. As you improve your Mutual Partnership through recovery, you have every reason to expect a mutually pleasurable sexual relationship as part of your improved interaction. After all, your sexual interaction is a powerful aspect of the total intercourse between you. So if you are living a life in recovery in which each day counts, one day at a time, it's not unreasonable to expect your sex life to count, too.

For sexual interaction to be mutually pleasurable on a regular basis, you will need to work together to create a positive, sexually intimate atmosphere, one that allows each of you to deliver your sexual messages honestly and openly. To create this positive, sexually intimate ambience, try to ensure the following as often as possible:

- Sufficient time for making love
- Privacy
- Confidentiality
- Acceptance of your (and your partner's) sexual identification and orientation
- Mutual respect and sensitivity to each other's feelings
- Absence of shame and guilt
- Freedom from fear—of unwanted pregnancy or of sexually transmitted infections or diseases
- Willingness to develop your (and your partner's) sexual skills

Both of you need to take mutual responsibility to nurture these positive elements. If you do, you will enhance your sexual intimacy and maximize your mutual satisfaction.

As you seek to improve your sex life with your Mutual

Partner, you will both embark on a sexually intimate journey. What you discover on this journey, only you and your partner will really know. But if you begin to take action, you will experience pleasurable results. Do you feel that you and your partner have some sexual adjustments to make? Would you both like to improve your sexual relationship in recovery? Good! Your reaffirmed commitment to your partner and your relationship will help promote sexual intimacy. And good, mutually gratifying sex thrives in an atmosphere of intimacy, an ambience that the emotional and spiritual development of recovery can only enhance.

SEXUAL PROBLEMS AND PERSPECTIVES

Sexual problems can spring from a wide variety of sources. Physical difficulties—ranging from anxiety, fatigue, or menstrual cycles to the aftereffects of an accident or disease—undeniably cause sexual problems. Some of the most common sexual problems include these:

1. *Lack of sexual desire:* disinterest in sex exhibited by one or both partners
2. *Impotence:* a man's inability to have or maintain an erection sufficient for intercourse
3. *Premature ejaculation:* a man's inability to control the timing of an orgasm
4. *Unresponsiveness:* a woman's inability to lubricate, to achieve sexual arousal, or to have an orgasm

Strictly physical causes can create all these sexual dysfunctions. But sex is not purely physical; it unites body, mind, and spirit. For this reason, sexual problems also often arise through a combination of psychological—mental and emotional—influences. Sporadic impotence, for example, almost always has psychological rather than physical roots. The old joke that the brain is the largest sexual organ actually hits pretty close to the mark. For just as easily as it can enhance sexual intimacy, the mind can create sexual problems. Low self-esteem, poor body image, fear of intimacy, other fears, anxiety, and guilt can all interfere with open and honest sexual expression. External factors, such as job stress, financial worries, or family pressures, can also create problems in your sex life. Sometimes, especially when a sexual problem persists, you may want to seek medical or psychological guidance or both. You may need professional treatment to help determine and overcome the source—physical or psychological—of the problem. But more often, you and your Mutual Partner can start to improve a sexual problem by making an effort to work on your relationship yourselves.

Because the kind of sex life you have largely depends on the type of relationship you have, the condition of your Mutual Partnership as a whole plays an enormous part in determining whether you will have sexual problems. For most people, the pleasure derived from sexual intimacy depends on the intimacy of the relationship. Since the physical aspect of making love—having sexual intercourse—provides only a fraction of your total sexual intimacy, it causes only a fraction of your sexual problems. The mental, emotional, and spiritual elements of your relationship, which strongly influence your sexual intimacy, also need to be explored in connection with your sexual problems.

Are sexual problems causing other problems in your relationship? Or are other relationship problems creating sexual conflict? Which came first, the chicken or the egg? Since your sex life is an integral part of your life as a whole, inextricably intertwined with every other aspect of love and intimacy, it makes little difference which came first. What goes on in the bedroom is direcly related to what happens in other parts of your home. Sexual problems *are* relationship problems. If you have one, you will almost definitely have the other, too. For most people, however, sexual problems provide something more tangible, and therefore easier to address, than other conflicts in their relationship. By starting to deal with these concrete sexual problems, however, you can sometimes identify and confront more widespread problems in your relationship.

Richard and Mary, married for five years and in recovery for almost three years, recently came to my office for help in dealing with a "sexual" problem. Richard complained that there was "not enough sex" in their marriage, while Mary felt that Richard was "selfish" and "unreasonable" in his sexual demands. He wanted her to show a little more affection; she wanted him to show a little more understanding. As you may have guessed, both partners felt angry and resentful with each other. But because they both had fallen into the trap of blaming each other, they neither explored nor discussed these feelings.

The biggest problem that Mary and Richard needed to face was a lack of communication in general, not merely an absence of sexual communication. What they really needed was not more sex, but more talk—which might then lead to better sex. During our first session, therefore, we focused on the importance of scheduling some "talk time." They both agreed that their equally frenetic schedules left little time to talk about sex —or anything else. They confessed that they "never had the chance" to sit down with each other and talk about what was important to them and what was happening in their lives. They hardly ever shared any of their feelings about life in general and about their sexual relationship in particular. Despite their hectic schedules, however, they decided to make a commitment to appropriate fifteen minutes a day when they could speak together without the usual distractions and interruptions. During this "talk time," they agreed to try to discuss any feelings that they had, not just about sex, but about anything important in their lives. I urged them to try to make "I" statements and to avoid criticizing or blaming each other. Doing so would ensure that they would use their time constructively and instructively without getting embroiled in a gripe session.

Richard and Mary took full advantage of the opportunity offered by this "talk time." Because they really listened to each other, their perceptions of each other and of their relationship started to change. Surprisingly, what started out as a discussion of a sexual problem quickly evolved into a discussion of their relationship as a couple and as a family. They shared their fears, resentment, anger, and feelings about themselves in addition to their thoughts about their sex life. And in doing so, Mary and Richard soon discovered that sex alone was not the problem.

Like most sexual complaints, their dissatisfaction turned out to be intertwined with other problems in their relationship. Mary felt somewhat overwhelmed by the competing pressures of her job, her eighteen-month-old baby, her household chores, and her relationship with her husband. She desperately wanted Richard's help and support in caring for their baby and their home. Because he never offered this kind of help, she felt underappreciated—and too tired and resentful to respond positively to his sexual advances. For his part, Richard no longer felt like a priority in Mary's life. He felt jealous and hurt because she always seemed to put the demands of her job and the needs of their baby before his needs. What he desperately wanted was some of her attention and affection, and he focused on her sexual unresponsiveness as a sign of her neglect in this regard.

Within a few couples sessions, Mary and Richard had come to understand a great deal about how the other felt. In the past, each had used anger to hide the hurt they didn't really know how to express. But when they agreed to put their anger and blaming aside, they became less defensive and adversarial. In honestly airing some of their hidden feelings for several weeks, they started to understand what each of them wanted and needed from their relationship as a whole. And they started to seek solutions together that would satisfy these needs. They became more positive, cooperative, and mutually supportive as a result of their improved communication. And this allowed them to work on making changes in their relationship in an atmosphere of negotiation and compromise.

Even though he had been raised to expect his wife to do all

the household chores, for example, Richard realized that it placed an unfair burden on a working wife and mother. He started to help out more with child care and suggested they get some outside help as well. They decided to hire a college student to clean their house once a week, which would relieve some of the time pressures that had made it difficult for them to devote much time to each other. And they agreed to spend this extra time together, doing things either as a couple or as a family. They planned intimate evenings together as well as family picnics.

Their "sexual" problem did not simply disappear, but it did start to fade as they worked on improving other parts of their Mutual Partnership. Richard became more sensitive to the times when Mary did not want to have sex because she felt exhausted, and he started to share household chores more in the evenings. As Mary felt less burdened and more helped by Richard, she became more affectionate and responsive. Since they took care of their household responsibilities more quickly by working together, they started going to bed earlier. The mutual effort spawned by their "talk time" had given them more time for sex. They felt more connected in every way: emotionally, spiritually, socially, mentally, and physically. And the intimacy they had created in every room of their home spread into the bedroom as well, yielding more deeply satisfying sexual experiences for both of them.

If you and your partner take the time to explore the connections between your sexual intimacy and the other aspects of your relationship, you, too, may find that "sexual" disagreements conceal other conflicts in your relationship. In an argument that ostensibly centers on sexual behavior or attitudes, you may actually be pursuing a hidden agenda. Like Mary and Richard, for example, you may want to win more attention and support through your sexual argument. Or you may allow a sexual disagreement to become the focus of a power struggle in your relationship. You may want to get "your way" to prove your self-worth, integrity, or superiority. You may feel competitive, combative, or controlling toward your partner in general.

To make sure you don't miss any of these connections, get into the habit of seeing your "sexual" problems in connection to your entire relationship. Try to think of sexual intimacy in its broadest context: as emotional, spiritual, and physical closeness. If you are having an argument about sex, for instance, you may find it enlightening to stop and consider other factors that may be contributing to your feelings of dissatisfaction. You may discover that nonsexual feelings have more relevance to your argument than does your sexual disagreement.

If you take the time to look at your sex lives, you will discover, as Richard and Mary did, that true sexual intimacy involves much more that an exchange of physical pleasure. All your deepest feelings, thoughts, opinions, fears, needs, and desires, as well as your physical pleasures, can come together in your sexuality. As you intimately exchange every aspect of yourselves, you will deeply enhance your sexual intimacy. Although important, physical pleasure forms merely the tip of the iceberg where sexual intimacy is concerned. So dive in and explore all that lies beneath the surface.

SEX TALK IS NOT A DIRTY WORD

Since sexual difficulties can usually be connected to relationship problems and most relationship problems involve a breakdown of communication, you may be able to avoid some sexual problems by improving your sexual dialogue. Indeed, as Mary and Richard discovered, shared communication can do more than anything else to improve your sexually intimate relationship and your sex life. Freely sharing sexual thoughts and feelings provides the basis for mutually satisfying sexuality, for just as it takes two people to have a sexual relationship in the first place, it takes two people, communicating openly and honestly, to solve sexual problems. Yet unless you first identify and verbalize your sexual difficulties, you will not be able to work together to solve them. You no longer need to feel afraid to confront sexual problems. After all, you already know that you can identify problems, work on them together, and resolve conflicts in other areas of your relationship. Approach sexual problems with the confidence that if you communicate openly and honestly with each other and apply the same principles of conflict resolution in this area, you can solve them together.

Sex is a mutual interaction of pleasure seeking, pleasure giving, and pleasure getting. Open and honest communication will increase your ability to give your partner the kind of pleasure she or he wants and enhance your opportunity to get from your partner the kind of pleasure you want. You need to nurture and support each other's sexuality through frank and honest exchanges. You have probably already developed a better understanding of your sexual self—your feelings, needs, thoughts, and desires. By combining this sexual self-awakening with your improved communications skills, you can do a lot to improve your sex life. Start by trying to share some of your sexual feelings, needs, and desires with your Mutual Partner, just as you have learned to share other intimate details of your life.

If you have never shared the intimate truth of your sexuality with your Mutual Partner before, you may find it difficult. Carla, one of my patients, had never talked about sex with her husband Jake in their seven years of marriage. Although she had never felt satisfied with their sex life, she had never complained. But after Jake had been in AA and Carla had been in Al-Anon and therapy for two years, she no longer felt comfortable pretending. She wanted to improve their sexual relationship, but she didn't know how to tell Jake that she got little enjoyment from their sexual intercourse.

"I seldom have an orgasm during intercourse, but I often fake it," Carla confesses, "because I want Jake to feel good about his sexual performance. I know that the sex will never get better unless I tell him the truth, but how can I admit now that I've been lying all this time? I really don't want to hurt him, and I know he'll get upset over this."

Carla had learned enough through her recovery to know

that she couldn't afford to stay in denial about their sex life or enable Jake to stay in his. But before she could confront him, she needed to overcome a common fear that prevents many people from talking about sexual dissatisfaction. Carla was afraid that if she told Jake how she really felt about their sex life, he would feel hurt or angry or both. She feared that if he felt hurt or angry enough, he might leave her. And these fears made her reluctant to take the risk of being rigorously honest about their lovemaking. Despite her fears, Carla eventually took the risk of sharing her feelings. She knew that after so many years, she had to acknowledge her own responsibility for her sexual dissatisfaction. She could no longer silently blame Jake for her lack of sexual orgasm, when she had never told him there was a problem.

"It wasn't easy for me," Carla continues, "but I did it. First, I tried to make Jake feel as comfortable as possible. I didn't want him to feel at all threatened by what I had to say. So I told him that I wanted us to be able to grow even closer together. I admitted that I hadn't been entirely truthful in the past. But I was afraid if I continued to hold back, we would never get as close as we could. He was still listening, so I guess I started out pretty good. Then I went on to say that I'd expected him to read my mind all these years, and I knew that was unfair. I needed to be more explicit about my sexual needs, so I wanted to know if Jake would be willing to talk about sex more. He seemed a little surprised, but he said, 'Great, let's do it.'

"So I just gulped and went ahead. I said what I would really enjoy was more hugging and kissing. I told him I wanted to show him some things he could do to help me have an orgasm more often. And I wanted to know how he felt, too, and how I could help make sex more satisfying for him. He asked me if I would take some more initiative, so I'm trying my best. I want to experiment a little more when we make love, so we're trying some new things, having some fun with it. It's been great so far. And Jake says he's having fun, too."

Neither Carla nor Jake felt fully comfortable during this first conversation about sex. But that talk was the icebreaker that both of them needed. Since Carla had approached it as a *mutual problem,* instead of finding fault with Jake, he didn't feel threatened or get defensive. They both wanted to make their sex life more satisfying, so they really listened to each other. As it turned out, Jake was actually quite receptive to the idea of talking about sex. Because they had never discussed it before, he had always assumed that Carla didn't like talking about sex. After this conversation, though, he started bringing it up himself. And they both started to put their words into action, by experimenting more with each other in bed, finding out what they liked through playful trial and error.

Having this kind of frank discussion outside the bedroom can make things much easier—and more gratifying—for both of you inside the bedroom. If you want someone else to try to satisfy you sexually, your best chance of getting what you want is to ask for it. Of course, simply asking for what you want is no guarantee that you will get it, but it will increase your odds enormously. So take the risk involved in communicating your sexual desires, feelings, and attitudes as honestly and openly as you do about other important matters in your Mutual Partnership. If you are unwilling to put your needs into words, you will have to depend on dumb luck to satisfy your needs.

Unfortunately, you may not find it easy to talk about sex at first. Since most people regard their sexuality as a private matter, many of us have difficulty talking about our sexuality, even with our intimate Mutual Partner. Like Carla and Jake, you may feel uncomfortable trying to open up a frank discussion of what sex and sexuality mean to each of you. If you work through your initial discomfort, though, as Jake and Carla did, you will find that the more you share, the more comfortable you will feel doing so. To get you both started, you may want to think about the following questions and then share your answers with your partner:

1. Do you accept your sexual identity and your individual sexuality?

2. Do you feel comfortable with your sexual views and values?

3. Do you enjoy the way you make love and the responsiveness of your body?

4. Are you sometimes spontaneous in enhancing your sex life, by breaking sexual routines or through sexual experimentation?

5. Do you talk about ways that you may improve your intimate times together?

6. Do you suggest new ways to express your love for each other?

7. Do you stay focused on making love while you're making love? (Or does your mind wander to other things?)

8. Do you make sex a priority in your life? (Or does it always come after work, family, and social responsibilities?)

9. Do you talk about sex outside the bedroom as well as in bed?

10. Do you tell your partner how much you love him or her and why?

11. Are you sensitive to your partner's feelings, attitudes, values, and inhibitions concerning sex?

12. Do you sometimes have sex even when you don't particularly feel like it, just because you care about your partner's needs?

13. Do you show and tell your partner what pleases or displeases you about your sexual activity?

14. Do you gently, clearly, and firmly ask for what you want sexually?

15. Do you accept sexual satisfaction as a reasonable expectation and intimate expression of your love?

16. Are you satisfied with your sex life?

If you answered yes to all these questions, then you already have a completely open and honest, sexually intimate Mutual Partnership. But if you answered no to any of them, follow each one up with a second question. Ask yourself: What are you willing to do to change no into yes? After seriously thinking about these questions and answering them honestly, share this exercise with your partner. Perhaps your partner would be receptive to thinking about these questions, too. By sharing this experience with each other, you will promote sexual intimacy by initiating a frank discussion of your sexuality. Use this exercise as a starting point for your own freewheeling discussions of sex and sexuality. Ask each other, for example, what you like best and least about your sex life. Try to make sure that your improved sexual intimacy involves give and take. After saying what you desire sexually, don't forget to ask your partner what she or he wants, too.

Despite the critical need for more sex talk, however, you'll both need to do more than talk. Remember that actions speak louder than words. After talking about sex, put what each of you has learned into practice in the bedroom (or the den, or the kitchen, or a deserted beach, or the backseat of a '57 Chevy). Have fun with your sexuality, trying new things until you find the activities and techniques that you like best.

Your sexual behavior is a potent means of communication, allowing you to express some of your deepest emotions to your partner. By improving your sexual communication—in words and in action—you will feel even more connected to your Mutual Partner physically, mentally, spiritually, and emotionally. Make a commitment to keep talking about sex and trying to improve your sexual intimacy. If you continue to communicate openly and honestly about your sexual desires, your sexual journey can be the most intimate experience of your relationship in recovery. If you are willing to put some time, effort, patience, tolerance, creativity, enthusiasm, and love into making your sex life as mutually satisfying as possible, you will create a special sexual relationship.

11

REATTACHMENTS

Reconnecting with Friends and Family

So far, you have probably concentrated on improving just one relationship: your relationship with the recovering alcoholic in your life. For many of you, that probably means a spouse or lover; but for others, it may be a parent, a sibling, or an adult child. By now, you have no doubt reaped the great rewards of self-improvement and the enhancement of your relationship with the recovering alcoholic. True and full recovery, however, demands more than improvement in just one relationship. To advance your recovery, you will need to reconcile with others as well, striving toward loving Mutual Partnerships in *all* your important relationships, not merely in your relationship with the recovering alcoholic.

Through your work in recovery, you have developed a new strength and a new capacity for love. Now you need to use that new strength and love to reach out to others. If you have been focusing on improving your relationship with your spouse, for example, you now need to turn your attention to relationships with your children, parents, siblings, and perhaps old friends. If, on the other hand, you have been concentrating your efforts on improving your relationship with another alcoholic relative—a parent or an adult child, for instance—you now need to move beyond that one relationship. By making the effort and putting in the work, you can build healthy relationships with all the people you know at home, at work, and at play.

Two people in recovery need to guard against "us-olation," the tendency to dive so deeply into one relationship that they close themselves off from the outside world. When alcoholism ruled your relationship, you may have shut out people, keeping your distance to prevent them from finding out your secret. In recovery, however, you need to open yourself and your relationship to others. For just as isolation limits your personal growth and the progress of your recovery, us-olation restricts the growth and recovery of your relationship as well as of yourself. By replacing isolation with us-olation, you will only perpetuate each other's codependency.

Do you still see the world as "us against them"? If you do, you're probably us-olating. Make sure you maintain a life outside your relationship with the recovering alcoholic. It's important that you both preserve your individuality and your individual connections with others. Don't let your "two-getherness" alienate you from other people. Instead, try to reconcile with some of the people—friends as well as family members—from whom you may have become estranged over the years.

These "outside" relationships may already have shown some improvement. Personal recovery and the recovery of one relationship tend to produce a ripple effect. Your personal transformation and the growth of your Mutual Partnership may have resulted in some changes in the ways you deal with others. Without really working at it, for instance, you have probably become more open and honest with other people, as well as with your Mutual Partner. But by actually directing your energies toward other relationships, you can further promote their improvement. You don't even have to learn anything new; all you really have to do is apply the lessons of recovery you have already learned to other areas of your personal life.

By expanding the scope of your work on relationship recovery, as the Twelfth Step of AA and Al-Anon urges, you will begin to practice the principles of recovery "in all [y]our affairs."

NOT QUITE MUTUAL PARTNERS: RECONCILING WITH CHILDREN

You probably share the same concerns about your children and reap the same rewards from your relationship with them that most other parents do. Because of the lingering influence of alcoholism, however, you will need to adopt some special approaches and strategies to provide your children with the special attention that children in recovery need. Whether the alcoholic was your spouse, sibling, or parent, the disease of alcoholism has undeniably affected you, and your codependency has no doubt influenced your children. And if the alcoholic had regular contact with your children—even as their grandparent, aunt, or uncle, but especially as one of their parents—then the disease affected them directly as well as indirectly. All relationships around an alcoholic tend to be strained and stained, and relationships with children are no exception. Children are also wounded by the disease of alcoholism.

Now that you and the alcoholic have a firm base of recovery, you'll need to work on reconciling with your children. You may not be able to make up for the "lost time" of the past, but you can take full advantage of the present to build better relationships with them. You already have access to all the tools you'll need. You have a new sense of self-esteem, one that you can impart to your children. In addition, you can apply your new respect, tolerance, and acceptance of others to your relationships with your children. You can establish a pattern of open and honest communication with them as you have done with the alcoholic. And you can work out resolutions to conflict and make peace. By applying all these familiar tools, you'll go a long way toward healing your relationships with your children.

"I was always confused about how to judge how we were doing with our kids," confesses Mitch, a machinist who has put a lot of work into restoring his relationship with his mother, a recovering alcoholic. "I realized that I really didn't know what a normal, happy family was supposed to do on a day-to-day basis. And Rebecca's dad is an alcoholic, too, so she didn't really know either. We felt like we were terrible parents, but we didn't know which way to turn. We used to stare at other families at the campground and at church and sort of compare what we did and said to the way they talked to each other. As it turned out, a lot of other parents didn't seem to know what they were doing either, but I never realized that until recently. The mystery of how to raise kids gradually went away once I got into a recovery program for my codependency, but I sometimes wished I had someone telling me what to do."

When you're raising children, it's hard not to make comparisons with other children and other families. But since there's no such thing as an "average" child, it rarely helps to make these kinds of comparisons. Remember that every child is a unique individual. So don't get stuck trying to compare your children to some abstract concept of "normal" behavior. "Normal" behavior covers a wide range—especially when you're dealing with children. Children grow up at different rates and in different ways. Each age will bring your children new opportunities, and each child has her or his own unique way of responding to those challenges.

Each age will bring you new challenges as a parent, too, and you will need to respond to them in the best way you know how. As you face the challenges of parenting, keep in mind that you don't need to be a perfect parent or have all the right answers all the time. When particular problems come up and you're not sure what to do, don't hesitate to ask for help. It may be hard for you to ask for help sometimes, but, remember, you didn't recover alone, and you don't have to develop your parenting skills in a vacuum either. Take advantage of the many opportunities around you that can help you learn how to solve parenting problems.

If you look for support in your parenting efforts, you may find it just around the corner. Meetings of AA and Al-Anon, as well as of Adult Children of Alcoholics, can offer you some terrific support as a parent in recovery. (And Alateen can provide your children with help in their own recovery.) In addition, most communities offer parenting discussion groups, courses, and workshops in a variety of settings—many at no cost or at low cost—while PTA meetings, by bringing you together with other parents, may be helpful, too. Friends, pediatricians, family therapists, scout leaders, books on parenting, and even your own parents may be valuable resources. Indeed, any resource you find that offers positive, reinforcing messages about parenting will serve you well as you struggle with the challenges of parenting.

Remember that individuals react differently to these various helpers. It may take a little time before you find a setting in which you and your partner feel comfortable. Try new parenting resources and discuss your feelings about them with your partner. By coming to your own conclusions, you will find the resources that are right for you. Even then, however, be discriminating before applying what you have heard to your own life. A method or parenting strategy that may have worked for one family may not be right for yours. So don't follow all the advice you hear; take what you can use and leave the rest.

REBUILDING TRUST

One of the first and biggest challenges you will need to face in improving your relationships with your children will be to try to rebuild their trust. The alcoholic's drinking and your codependent reactions may have made it difficult for your children to trust you both. A long trail of erratic behavior and broken promises may have left them with shattered dreams and shattered spirits. Perhaps Dad, always focusing on Mom's drinking, was inconsistent in showing his affection to the children. Or maybe Grandpa, preoccupied with his drinking, never followed through on his promises to take the children to the zoo. After so much hurt, it may take a while before the children are willing to forgive and forget. And no matter how long it takes, you will probably experience it as an eternity. After all, *you* know how much you have recovered. You may wonder why your children can't see it, too.

But even if you think you have become more open and honest now, your children may hesitate before they become equally open and honest. They may remain silent, sullen, suspicious, and scared for a while. No matter how secure you feel in your recovery, they may not feel the same way. So try not to be impatient while you try to win back your children's trust. Acknowledge that both you and the alcoholic—whether she or he is the children's parent, grandparent, aunt, uncle, or sibling—probably gave your children plenty of reasons *not* to trust you. Schooled in distrust, they may think that recovery is just another promise, and they are waiting for it to be broken. For this reason, don't be surprised if your children test and retest you. They will want to find out whether you have really changed and whether you finally mean what you say. In addition, your children might display resentment or anger at losing their former caretaking/parenting roles.

SETTING LIMITS

Like most children, they will probably put you through the greatest test when you try to set limits and impose restrictions on their behavior. Making and enforcing family rules and regulations will by no means be an easy task. You will find, however, that in an atmosphere of negotiation and compromise with your partner, you will come up with a reasonable set of rules to present to your children. You and your children need to understand clearly "who's responsible for what." All the family members need to know what's expected of them, so they clearly know what you consider right and wrong behavior and what you regard as their responsibilities. Of course, as situations change, rules may need to change, too. And as your children get older, you may want to include them in the process of negotiation and compromise, working out flexible rules together. But at other times, you as a parent will have no choice but to lay down the law, *without* involving your children in the decision making. As a parent, you have the ultimate responsibility and, therefore, the final authority to make the rules in your home. And in addition to knowing their responsibilities, your children need to know who's in charge.

Whatever rules you make, you can reasonably expect your children to break one or two of them at times. Few children obey all the rules all the time. For this reason, you and your children also need to know what to expect when they break rules. In establishing rules of behavior or discipline, you will find that consistency, cooperation, and communication in a calm setting will produce the most positive results. Together, you and your partner need to work out the consequences of broken rules and then communicate them to your children *before* they actually break the rules. That way, if your children break a rule or two, both you and they will know what to expect.

In setting down rules of behavior and discipline, you and your partner will need to present a united front to your children. If your children see two parents acting as a solid unit, resisting their attempts to divide or manipulate the parents, they will take notice. Once they see that trying to pit one parent against the other doesn't work, they'll soon stop trying. Your united front as parents will impart an important message of clarity and consistency to them. As your children become aware that you mean what you say and that you both stand together in saying it, they will begin to respect your wishes.

DRUG AND ALCOHOL USE

Among the most important rules you will need to establish in your family are those about drug and alcohol use. As stories about children using drugs and alcohol at earlier and earlier ages fill the pages of our newspapers, the concern about children and drugs has become uppermost in most parents' minds. From your personal experience, you already know that addiction can wreak enormous destruction. Knowing that children of alcoholics and addicts have a high risk of becoming addicted themselves, you will certainly want your children to develop a keen understanding of the nature of addiction and recovery. Above all, of course, you would like to prevent your children from becoming addicted to drugs and alcohol themselves. But you may feel puzzled about how and when to talk to your children about drugs and alcohol.

Unfortunately, there are no magic formulas that determine when you should begin talking to your children about addiction. It's never too early to start educating your children about drug use. But the age of your children and your own progress in recovery will influence the way that you communicate your knowledge, experience, and concerns to them. Here again, you may benefit from seeking help from outside resources. Most schools, for instance, employ counselors who know about addictions, and many schools have begun to institute educational programs about drugs and alcohol.

Whatever formal education your children receive concerning alcohol and other drugs, however, you can supplement their education by sharing your own experience of alcoholism, codependency, and recovery with them. In recovery, you need to commit yourself to the idea and practice that family secrets are a thing of the past. Since recovery is important to you, you will naturally want your children to know and understand your involvement in Al-Anon or AA or both. It doesn't mean that you should saturate them with the steps and slogans of your recovery program, language that your children may find foreign. But it does mean that you should openly and honestly acknowledge the existence of drug and alcohol abuse and share your profound understanding of the problem with your children.

No matter how vigilantly you tackle the issue of drugs, you need to be realistic. Wherever you live, your children will see and hear a lot about drug use. Since drinking and drug abuse continue to spread across the country, you cannot protect your children from exposure to drug use. The best you can do is establish reasonable, loving, and clear-cut rules with your children. Let them know exactly what you expect of them as far as drug and alcohol use are concerned. But try not to go overboard. Trying to enforce unrealistic and overprotective rules, such as refusing to allow your children to go to any parties, will not work. Of course, ignoring the problem by avoiding discussions of drinking at parties won't work either. Both strategies fail to prepare your children for the *reality* of drug and alcohol abuse. You need to open your children's eyes to the reality of drug use and do your best to prepare them for real-life situations, so they will know what to do when they actually need to confront the problem (as most children will).

While continuing to do your best to educate your children about drugs and alcohol, guard against the resurrection of denial. Most parents, whether in recovery or not, have an instinctive response to the possibility of drug use by their children: "Not my kids!" Despite your recovery, you have no special protection from this kind of denial where your children are concerned. Keep your eyes open and try to develop a balanced view. Try to avoid seeing drug and alcohol problems everywhere, as some parents in recovery do, but at the same time, don't shut your eyes to the possibility that your children will abuse drugs. If you have serious questions about your children and drugs, turn to others—teachers, guidance counselors, professionals, and people in your recovery program—who can offer you knowledgeable and perceptive assistance.

In educating your children about drugs and alcohol, remember that you have a unique set of strengths that you can bring to bear on this issue. As a person who has overcome alcoholism or codependency or both, you will set a powerful example for your children. You've learned to nurture a full and loving life, free of addiction, codependency, and other destructive patterns. Since you cannot exercise absolute control over your children, you cannot *force* them to avoid drug and alcohol use. But if you openly share your own lives with them, your children will probably follow your lead.

In drugs, as in everything else, what you tell your children will not matter nearly as much as what they see you do. Remember that you and your partner are your children's first and most influential role models. For this reason, your children will probably do what you do more often than they will do what you say. Don't become obsessed with the idea of becoming a "perfect" role model, but try to be as good a role model as you possibly can. Naturally, you will make some mistakes and need to improve. But by admitting your parenting mistakes and learning from them, you will become a better and better parent. And your children, in observing you, will learn how to handle their mistakes openly and honestly. They will recognize that life follows a path of constant learning and will begin to follow that path themselves.

RESPECTING YOUR CHILDREN'S INDIVIDUALITY

Although they may follow your lead, remember also that your children are individuals, destined to choose their unique path through life. Just as you needed to establish secure boundaries between yourself and the recovering alcoholic, you also need to form clear-cut boundaries between yourself and your children. And you will need to demonstrate respect for those boundaries—and for your children—through your interaction. You will need to strike an often-precarious balance between underinvolvement and overinvolvement in your children's lives.

"My thirteen-year-old looks just like I did at her age, and I see a lot of myself in her," admits Yvonne, the mother of three children. "So when she turned down a scholarship to a summer art program, I just went nuts. I would have died for that kind of opportunity when I was a teenager. But despite my feelings, I managed to keep my cool. And that allowed me to come to terms with the fact that this art program obviously meant more to me than it meant to Jennifer. And that's okay. If it's not the most important thing in the world to her, I don't see why she should do it. I don't think I would have been able to say that a few years ago, but I've grown a lot since then."

Yvonne made a wise choice in not blowing up when her daughter made a decision that surprised her. She realized that despite any physical, intellectual, or temperamental similarities, she and her daughter were *not* the same person. In growing up, your children, like Jennifer, will develop their own set of interests and priorities. And though you can offer them encouragement, support, and sometimes guidance, you cannot choose every aspect of their life for them. If you truly respect your children and the differences between you and them, you will exercise a little self-restraint at times, allowing them to choose their own way.

As long as you remain loving, emotionally available, and sensitive to the feelings and needs of your children, you will be a good parent. Of course, no matter how good you are, you can always become a better parent. After all, since nobody's perfect, we all have room to improve. So take a moment to consider your relationship with your children. See how many of these guidelines for positive parenting you observe.

BUILDING SELF-ESTEEM

- Do you show and tell your children that you love them?
- Do you devote individual time to each child?
- Do you play or have fun with your children, whatever their ages?
- Are you an attentive listener and a strong supporter of your children's concerns?

- Do you try not to embarrass your children by criticizing them in public or by teasing or ridiculing them?
- Do you keep your voice in a conversational tone even when you feel angry or upset? Do you try not to nag, yell, or threaten?
- Do you treat your children with patience and tolerance and try not to blame them?

RESPECTING YOUR CHILDREN'S RIGHTS AND BOUNDARIES

- Do you show them that you respect them and that they have rights?
- Do you allow your children some privacy?
- Are you involved in your children's activities without becoming overinvolved or underinvolved?
- Are you careful not to fight your children's battles for them or bail them out of trouble when they should be learning to accept responsibility?
- Do you protect your children from being saddled with your burdens?
- Do you free children from taking on too much responsibility?
- Do you encourage and help your children to establish meaningful relationships with people—friends and other relatives—outside your immediate family?

COMBINING AUTHORITY AND AVAILABILITY

- Do you set limits and stick to them?
- Are you an authority figure without being a dictator?
- Do you encourage your children to come to you with their problems?
- Do you provide a safe environment in which your children feel free to express their feelings?
- Do you nurture and guide your children to the best of your ability?

ENCOURAGING TRUST, OPENNESS, AND HONESTY

- Do you let your children know—through actions as well as words—that they can now trust you?

- Do you provide a role model of openness and honesty to your children?
- Do you behave reliably, consistently, and courteously?
- Do you admit your own humanness, your wrongs, and say you're sorry when you've made a mistake?

If you answered no to any of these questions, then you have pinpointed an area in which you could improve as a parent. By working to develop these basic tools, you can become a better parent. You will help build your children's self-esteem, encourage them in their various efforts, establish clear-cut rules and expectations, and rebuild the trust between you.

Despite these guidelines, as you will discover, good, positive parenting does not come from any book. Every parenting situation presents unique challenges, which neither you nor any book can accurately predict. So try not to project what you will do if this happens or that happens. Just tackle each day and each new set of problems as they arise, moment by moment. If your work at it, day by day, you will find that good parenting springs from your courage, love, patience, and understanding. By nurturing these qualities in yourself, you will transform yourself into a good parent. Take a moment to think about all the things you have to offer your children in recovery: love, affection, reliability, consistency, responsibility, comfort, support, tolerance, and encouragement. These strengths, which recovery has helped you acquire or bolster, are the greatest gifts you can offer your children—gifts that no amount of money could ever buy.

RECONCILING WITH FRIENDS AND ADULT FAMILY MEMBERS

During the period when you were caught up in the alcoholism of someone you loved, you may have developed distant or strained relationships with friends and nonalcoholic members of your family. You may have cut yourself off from some of these people because you didn't want "outsiders"—even other members of your family—to know about the addiction and all the trouble it had caused you. You might have feared their disapproval or rejection. Perhaps you thought that others didn't really care enough about you to want to know when things started to get rough. Or maybe you just thought that nobody else could possibly understand what addiction—and later recovery—was all about.

But having come this far in recovery, your perspectives of yourself, the world, and the people in it may have changed enormously. Ask yourself where you are *now* in recovery, and where your family members and oldest friends are. Taking a fresh look at the people you once knew best, and who knew you best in return, may yield new insights into both them and you. You may even find that both you and they are now willing to behave differently toward one another. And reconnecting with family and friends can enrich both your lives and theirs.

Significant others can make a major difference in the way you solve both everyday and once-in-a-lifetime problems. As you attempt to adjust to the various trials and stresses that occur throughout life, long-standing relationships—among old and dear friends or among family members—can provide you with a great deal of support. By setting up a support system made up of extended family members and close friends, you can provide yourself with a safeguard against the unexpected stresses and strains that may develop as you continue on your path toward recovery. And since Mutual Partnerships work both ways, you will provide your friends and family with the same kind of safeguard.

Investing in your friendships and your family can provide both you and them with a tremendous source of strength. The love and nurture you receive from your family and friends can increase your sense of security in yourself and in your relationships, and this sense of security will help you deal with life's inevitable struggles. The collective strength represented by a bond among friends or family members can provide you with formidable force on your side. Two of my friends in recovery added this recognition of mutual support to their wedding ceremony. As part of their marriage vows, they called upon their friends and family members for support and encouragement, "to help us in our efforts to nurture a love that reaches out to others, a love dedicated to more than just our own happiness." Their stated commitment to each other encompassed a unity with others outside their Mutual Partnership.

Are you still reluctant to reconcile with family members and old friends? Despite the great strides you have made in your recovery, you still may not feel comfortable sharing your life with old friends and relatives. You may feel reluctant to pursue reconciliation for any or all of the following reasons:

- You may want to keep your recovery—and the alcoholic's —strictly anonymous.
- You may not trust other people—friends and family members alike—to appreciate the ways in which your life has changed.
- Your friends or relatives may drink, take drugs, or be mired in their own codependent relationships themselves.
- You may have some lingering shame about the family disease that makes you doubt whether you should share your secrets.
- You may feel ambivalent about how much contact you want and how much emotional energy you want to expend on relationships "from the past."
- You may be hanging on to old resentments and not be ready to make amends with old friends and other family members.
- You may be afraid of reconciling.
- You may not know where to begin in reconciling with friends and family members.

All these reasons are valid. Indeed, in the early days of recovery, when you still felt tentative about yourself and your improvement, you may have been wise not to attempt a reconciliation for any of these reasons. If your family members or old friends were part of their own actively alcoholic environment, for instance, reconnecting with them might have knocked you and your recovery off balance. Even now, though you feel more secure in your recovery, it may be prudent to keep your distance from certain relatives and friends who seem overly intrusive, in denial themselves, or in any way threatened by your recovery.

"When Keith first got sober, we needed to distance ourselves from my family even though I would have loved their support," admits Renée, who felt that her parents might endanger her recovery as well as her husband's. "My father was still drinking heavily at the time, so I felt really uncomfortable around them. They were so deep in their own denial that they denied Keith's problem with alcohol, too. There was just no way they could be supportive of our Twelve-Step activities. I tried a few times at first, telling them that Keith had stopped drinking and was going to AA meetings and that I had started going to Al-Anon. But they said things like, 'He never drank that much.' And a few weeks later they asked me, 'Are you still going to *those* meetings?' I found myself getting so uptight around them that I figured it was threatening my recovery. I needed support, not criticism. So I felt it was best for me to have minimal contact with them."

Renée made the right choice in keeping her distance from her parents in the early days of her recovery. Her father's drinking and her mother's codependency tended to revive some of her own codependent patterns of behavior, the old patterns that she was trying so hard to put behind her. Like many heavy drinkers and their partners, Renée's parents had little tolerance or sensitivity for their son-in-law's new, fragile sobriety or their daughter's concerns. Their persistent denial sometimes even created doubt in Renée's mind about whether Keith really had an alcohol problem. Under conditions like these, it would have damaged her and set back her recovery to attempt any sort of in-depth reconciliation. Fortunately for Renée, however, times change and people change with them.

"Something truly amazing happened in the past six months. My father went through an on-the-job intervention and was sent to a rehab center, and my mother started going to Al-Anon, too. They're totally different people today. I feel like we're really talking for the first time in many, many years. We're getting to know each other on a whole different level. And now that I see my parents in recovery, instead of stuck in the disease, I can be much more forgiving. I don't dread family get-togethers anymore.

"I still have to hold back a little, though. It's tempting to want to 'sponsor' their recovery in a way, by telling them all about our recovery and making all sorts of suggestions. But I know they have their own sponsors. They only just started their recovery, and they still have a long way to go. But they'll get there without my advice. I hope we'll get closer, too, but that'll come, if it comes, one day at a time."

Once her parents got into recovery, the tension between Renée and them disappeared. Their own recovery had started to transform their attitudes, putting them on the same wavelength as their daughter and son-in-law. For her part, Renée had good reason to want to reconcile with her family. "After all, your family is your family for life," she explains. She wanted to put the past behind her and give both herself and her parents a second chance to try to build a more constructive, mutually supportive relationship.

Still, despite their recovery, Renée continued to maintain a certain distance between herself and her parents. Her long history with her parents made it too easy for her to slip back into old patterns of behavior that made her feel anxious and angry. She still felt too vulnerable in their presence to be entirely comfortable with them. Even though they had become much more supportive and understanding, Renée realized that she needed to erect some firm boundaries between herself and her family. For the sake of everyone involved, they had to work out a comfortable balance between closeness and distance. As Renée recognized, in reattaching to others—especially to those who either have an addiction or are in recovery from addiction or codependency—you will need to guard against codependent overinvolvement.

Renée's husband Keith had a slightly different experience in his efforts to reattach to others. An only child, Keith had lost both his parents before he sobered up. Although he could not reconcile with his family, he had also drifted apart from several close friends during the time he was drinking heavily. After so many years of alienation, he badly wanted to reconnect with these friends. Unfortunately, with some of his friends, Keith found that he had to put the brakes on.

"I'm trying now to reestablish a closer relationship with some of my oldest friends, but I'm proceeding with caution," Keith explains. "Chip and Adam, we go way back, all the way to junior high school, when we were like the three musketeers. But they're still drinking pretty heavily themselves, so I can't do much with them. I did tell them I'm in AA, and I offered to take them to a meeting if they ever want to go. But when they start drinking, we go our separate ways.

"Things are going much better between me and Clare. She and I also go back a long way, but we're getting much closer than we ever were before. She even works with me now at the firm—I gave her a job because she said she really needed to get out of the house. Her husband's a really heavy hitter as far as drinking goes. She asks us lots of questions about the disease, and she's learning a lot about her codependency. She and Renée have been going to Al-Anon meetings together for a couple of months and Clare also went to an open AA meeting with me. Last week, she asked me if her son Randy could go to an Alateen meeting with our daughter Lori. So we're getting more involved with her and her family, and we both think that's great."

In trying to reconcile with his old friends, Keith discovered that some of those who still drank a lot were not ready or willing to think about cutting down or stopping. So to protect himself, Keith decided to maintain a flexible distance from Chip and Adam. He found that he could still enjoy their company when they were sober, but whenever their drinking started to escalate, Keith would leave them behind. Fortunately, his friendships with other people from his past continued to grow, providing him with a sense of satisfaction and reconnection with his history.

As Keith did, you may discover that you have to practice a type of "selective reattachment." It may sound harsh, but you will need to be careful about reconnecting to family members or friends who may still have drinking problems. If these people continue to behave compulsively or addictively, you may find that spending too much time with them could prove hazardous to your health—and to your recovery. You will need to acknowledge that you can't force other people to recognize their problems and take the Twelve Steps. The best you can do, as Keith did, is to leave the door open, letting them know that if they want help for their problems, they know where to find you.

If you tend to allow friends and family members to become overly intrusive, as Renée did, or you have a tendency to become overinvolved in their lives, as Keith did, you may have to place some limits on your involvement with them. You may not find it easy to set limits with your friends and family members. You may feel guilty about "abandoning" them when they so "obviously" need you. But you can't really help them if overinvolvement in each other's lives prevents you from growing the way you want to grow. Instead of vainly trying to please all these people all the time, you need to work on redefining your boundaries. You may find that you can actually offer your family and friends more by becoming stronger through your recovery. So try to practice saying no as a complete sentence. That will help you keep your boundaries exactly where you want them: where they will allow you to grow the most.

"Buying furniture for our new home really brought out some boundary problems with my mother," admits Eliza. "You see, my mother buys old houses, fixes them up, and then sells them. She's made quite a good living doing this for over twenty-five years, and she really does have a lot of talent. Of course, she has some very definite ideas about what our house should look like. But she doesn't seem to understand that her taste is not the same as ours.

"Roger and I agreed that we had to stick to our guns, no matter how much she tried to influence us. She would actually go so far as to buy a piece of furniture for us, saying she couldn't resist because it was 'just right' for our house. Sometimes the piece wasn't even that horrible, but that wasn't the point. We wanted to choose our own furniture together. And we knew if we gave in on one stick of furniture, she'd want to furnish the whole house. So we came up with a standard reply that we had ready whenever she appeared on our doorstep with the 'perfect' piece of furniture. It goes something like this: 'Mom, this is a really lovely end table, and you got it for a very good price, but it's not exactly what we're looking for. We do appreciate your interest, but we want to look for our own furniture. We know you'll understand how important it is for our home to reflect *our* particular style.' That approach seemed to get through to her. Oh, we may have had to bypass one or two things that we could have lived with, but we knew it was better for us to hold our ground and just say, 'No, thank you.' "

Eliza and Roger managed to set a clear boundary with her mother and present it to her mother in a firm but kind way. They understood that reconciliation sometimes means moving farther apart. If being too close to a family member or friend starts to make you feel a little crazy at times, you need to say or do something about it. You may need to work on establishing a boundary that will allow you to remain connected to the other person without feeling overwhelmed. As Robert Frost wrote, "Good fences make good neighbors." You may need to build an appropriate fence between you and your neighbors. Unfortunately, as you will surely discover, setting boundaries with friends can be just as difficult as setting boundaries with family members.

"My friend Fred has been in AA for ten months. Now, he's always calling me up to see if I want to go to a meeting," complains Jordan, an adult child of an alcoholic parent who has worked hard in recovery to establish a Mutual Partnership with his mother. "He always knows the 'best' meeting, the 'best' sponsor, the 'best' speaker. I keep telling him that for now, ACOA is the only program I need. I may be wrong;

maybe he's right in thinking I have a problem with alcohol. But his goading isn't going to get me into AA. So I finally told him that yes, I sometimes think I drink too much, but that's not saying I admit that I'm 'powerless over alcohol and my life is unmanageable.' I appreciate his concern, but I really resent his heavy-handedness. My boozing is my business, not his. I guess I'll just have to keep telling him that until he backs off."

Don't be surprised if it takes considerable practice before you feel truly comfortable telling your friends and family members what you think and feel. But don't worry, they will probably give you plenty of opportunity to practice. Since they may not be used to hearing you say what you feel, as Jordan found out, you may have to repeat the same message over and over until the person finally hears and accepts it. By getting your friends and family members to listen to your words, even when those words are demanding more space, you will inevitably further the process of reconciliation and recovery.

MOVING TOWARD RECONCILIATION

If you've decided that the time is right for you to reconcile with some of your friends and family members, you can start right away. With some of your old friends and certain members of your family, it may take nothing more than a phone call to start things up again. Set a time to make a call or pay a visit to someone you love, but haven't talked to for a while. You may want to start with nothing more than a five-minute phone conversation in which you try to talk about your feelings and encourage the other person to return the favor. Even if you never really allowed yourself to talk, feel, or trust in your relationship with these people before, you can add those qualities to your relationships with them today. It will just take a little practice; you'll get the hang of it quick enough. If you try to practice this kind of honesty once a week for several weeks (or even once a month for several months) in a particular relationship, you may see a startling return on your investment. Your friend, or your father, or your sister, may begin sharing his or her feelings with you on a regular basis, too. If you can make this kind of mutual interaction an established pattern, your relationship—and both of you as individuals—will undoubtedly grow.

Reconciliation sometimes demands more than merely reaching out to another person. Sometimes it requires you to make amends for past injuries. You probably have already made amends to some people in connection with the Ninth Step of AA and Al-Anon. Perhaps you made direct amends through a verbal apology. In addition, you may have made changes in your attitudes or behavior—showing more tolerance, understanding, and acceptance, for example—that reflect your desire to correct past wrongs. In certain situations, however, you may not feel totally comfortable trying to mend certain fences face to face. In such a case, you may discover that writing letters can be a valuable tool of reconciliation.

You can use letter writing in two different ways, both of which tend to promote reconciliation. You may choose to write a letter, but not actually send it. You may not need to make amends; you may merely need to express yourself. In such cases, the simple act of setting your thoughts down on paper can prove therapeutic. By airing your feelings, even if you never share them with anyone else, you may process past events in a new way. The new insights that may result from this letter-writing exercise may make it easier for you to forgive yourself and others whom you love for past wrongs. In that way, you may come to a satisfactory personal resolution of an old wound. And this resolution, in itself, can promote reconciliation.

Writing a letter that you actually send to someone else, however, signals a willingness to make amends, to change for the better and enter an improved relationship. By saying on paper what you may find too difficult to express aloud, you will send a clear message to the person you love. And this kind of meaningful correspondence can truly revive and improve your relationship in recovery.

Gordon and William, lovers for ten years, have been in recovery for the past three years. They agreed that it was important to their Mutual Partnership for each of them to build a secure network of family and friends outside their relationship. So after attaining sobriety, Gordon spent considerable time visiting and writing his father, from whom he had felt distant in the past. Their recent exchange of letters provides a moving testimony to the power of reconciliation:

Dear Dad:
   This is a letter which every son should have the privilege to write his father.
   I am proud you are my father. We are more similar than different, you and I. Among other things, I have inherited your skill with things technical (although you apply yours in science and I in the law), your love of music, your fine, analytical mind, and your honest intellect.
   I know that my being gay was painful for you and Mother to accept and for that pain I am sorry. It took us time to understand that none of us had any choice in that turn of fate. I was wild and irresponsible as a young man and that hurt you, too. I apologize for that and hope I have redeemed myself in the years that followed.
   You gave me life and nurtured me. I appreciate the magnitude of that job, now, and your restraint when Grandmother interfered. You taught me, mostly by example, an ethic of gentle kindness and generosity. You provided me with a fine education, but more, you set me an example by which to live my adult life. Daily in me I see you and hear you, for I am largely modeled upon you.
   I am grateful for all you have done for me.
   I respect and love you.
                                                    Gordon

Dear Gordon:
   I am grateful to you for your very communicative letter and for the assurance put into words of what I mean to you. I guess that I sensed what you said, but couldn't be sure.
   You should also know, in words, of my pride in you and my admiration of you. Of course I see much of me in you and

naturally believe that to be good. Beyond your music, law skills, analytic skills, and intellect, I observe a man who displays honesty, dignity in living, and great concern for interacting with and helping others. In particular, I am pleased at your interest and concern with Susan and Barbara and their families. I am sure that they also value this.

It worried me that I might have failed you in not providing a sufficiently strong father figure, or that I did not devote enough time to being a father. . . . I agonized that our behavior might have contributed strongly. . . . Whatever the cause, I know that being gay puts a heavy burden on a person. I believe that you have handled it with honesty and dignity and have carved out an honorable life of which we can all be proud. Your career as a lawyer has been spectacular.

I have great respect (and I shouldn't be surprised) for your conquering alcoholism and your continuing efforts in that field.

I respect and love you also.   Dad

Although Gordon received an extremely positive response from his father, you may not always get the same kind of reaction. More often than not, as you will discover if you try, your family members and old friends will respond warmly to your conciliatory overtures. But you shouldn't count on it. If you want to make an effort at reconciliation, simply because it will make you feel better about your relationships and because you want to do everything you can to improve them, then do it. But don't automatically assume that you will get an equal return on your investment. The sincerity of your motives, more than anything else, will increase the chances that your friends and family will reciprocate—if only you will take the initiative.

Paradoxically, having a long history with family members or old friends makes it both easier and harder to reconcile. Since you have known them for so long, it may be easier to know what kind of behavior to expect in response to your advances. Yet, at the same time, you may find it harder to make those overtures in the first place. You may have built up walls of resentment and resistance that you can only take down slowly and carefully. Or you and the other person may have become so settled in your patterns of interaction that it may seem as if it requires a superhuman effort to break away from those patterns. Actually, though, all it really requires is love. Because you are in a loving program, you probably know more about love than you realize. Your capacity to love, growing through recovery, can help heal a great number of old wounds and move you toward reconciliation. If you surrender to it, your love will allow you to develop a new intimacy with all the people you have ever loved.

NEW RELATIONSHIPS, NEW FRIENDSHIPS, NEW INTIMACY

Recovery, as AA and Al-Anon teach, offers a "bridge back to life." On the other side of that bridge, you will find an improved relationship not only with the recovering alcoholic, but with your children, parents, other relatives, and close friends. But the improvement of your relationships need not end with old friends and old family members. For as you continue to grow in recovery, your family will continue to expand as well. Through marriage or living with another person, you may widen your family network. Or perhaps other family members may do the same, bringing you new in-laws, nieces, nephews, stepparents, and grandchildren. At the same time, your circle of friends will most likely expand. You may add new friends to the friends you already made when you were an Eye-Opener, those you made later when you were a Pioneer, and those from the past with whom you've now reconciled. Some of these new friendships you may share with your Mutual Partner, while others will be yours alone. Yet you can cultivate intimacy among new friends as well as old and among new family members as well as old. By continuing to work at it, you will find that your recovery can lead to more meaningful connections with all the people who become part of your life.

Your choice of new friendships may reveal a great deal about you. Like most people, you will probably tend to pick friends whose values, interests, and outlook are not so different from yours. Remembering the past misery of your codependency, though, try to choose your friends wisely. A great many afflictions in life—depression, negativity, desperation, and dependency—can become contagious. As a veteran of codependency and victimization, you may need to guard against spending too much time and energy with active alcoholics, codependents, and victims. Certainly, in accordance with the Twelfth Step, you will want to devote some time in trying to "carry this message to others"—helping active codependents and alcoholics open their eyes to their illness and get the help they need. Yet at the same time, you will need to strive to balance these relationships by forming others that have the power to nourish you as you nourish others.

Mutual Partners can have a lot of fun while making new friends in recovery. You may not even have to expend a lot of effort in actively looking for new friendships. Simply start doing things that you both like to do and invariably, you will run into other people who like doing the same or similar things. Expand the horizons of your social life. You may want to take up square dancing, or perhaps ballroom dancing is more your style. You may want to join a swim club or a health spa, go hiking with a group, or join a new church or synagogue. All these activities will offer you opportunities to meet new people, while you have fun with an activity that you enjoy.

Recovery is not always easy. At times, it may seem as if it might be easier to hide out in your recovery program, hibernate alone at home, or us-olate with your partner. But if you give life a chance, you can have some fun with it. You've worked hard at recovery and should feel good about your progress. But recovery, like life itself, should not always be so serious. So don't forget to play with recovery, too. By building a new social life, you will discover some of the fun and joy of recovery.

LOVE IS THE ANSWER

Your life has already improved dramatically. You have trusted the process of recovery, and you have worked hard to make that process work for you. By now, you have undoubtedly enhanced your physical, mental, emotional, and spiritual health. You should feel proud and pleased with your progress in recovery. You have fought to survive—and you won!

Through recovery, you have acquired new knowledge and awareness, changed your attitudes, begun to accept life on life's terms, and taken positive actions to improve your life. You now recognize your life is valuable because you know you have intrinsic worth as a person. Your increased self-esteem now permits you to find pleasure for yourself, rather than suffering for others. You no longer feel pressed to rescue or fix everyone else, while ignoring your own needs. Although you no longer automatically take the bait when people try to lure you into your old codependent patterns of behavior, you do treat people with support and sensitivity, caring and compassion. And because you no longer feel isolated and alone, you celebrate each day as a gift and a challenge to make it really count. All these improvements have allowed you to make—and continue to make—great strides in all your relationships: old and new, with family members and friends.

Love—of yourself as well as of others—has made all things possible. Love has become the basis of your recovery and all your relationships. Recovery has afforded you a new life, one that has allowed love—your own love and the love offered by others—to transform you miraculously. Reconciliation and reaching out have multiplied the number of relationships you have in recovery and have added to the quality of their intimacy. Love had made all this possible. Whatever the problem has been, love has been the answer. And love will always be the answer.

RESOURCE ORGANIZATIONS

When you seek information on treatment for addictions or problems related to dysfunctional families, start with the local telephone book or contact an agency that is a central clearinghouse for services in your local area. The addresses and telephone numbers listed here are those of the national headquarters of selected organizations. Some of these organizations provide hotline counseling; others offer referrals to services in your area, as well as informational and educational materials.

Al-Anon Family Group Headquarters
1372 Broadway (at 38th Street)
7th Floor
New York, NY 10018
800–245–4656; in the New York area, 212–302–7240

Callers receive information about Al-Anon meetings in their area; a catalog of free literature and videotapes is offered free of charge; literature is sent at low fees. Also sponsors Alateen.

Alateen

Call Al-Anon. Refers children, ages 11–18, whose lives are affected by alcoholism, to groups.

Alcoholics Anonymous—General Service Office (AA)
468 Park Avenue South
New York, NY 10016
212–686–1100

Refers callers to AA meetings in their areas; has a free catalog of literature and pamphlets, books, and videotapes at a low cost.

American Anorexia/Bulimia Association, Inc.
133 Cedar Lane
Teaneck, NJ 07666
201–836–1800

Offers callers referrals to clinicians who specialize in eating disorders;
newsletter costs $25.00 per year (five issues), free reading lists.

American Association for Marriage and Family Therapy
1717 K Street, N.W.
Washington, DC 20006
202–429–1825

Referral source for locating qualified marital and family therapists in the
United States and Canada.

Children of Alcoholics Foundation
200 Park Avenue
31st Floor
New York, NY 10016
212–351–2680

Offers a packet of general information free of charge; makes referrals to
groups and treatment programs throughout the country; and sends special reports for a small charge.

Cocaine Anonymous—National Office
PO Box 1367
Culver City, CA 90232
213–559–5833

Hotline gives referrals to Twelve-Step groups.

Debtors Anonymous
PO Box 20322
New York, NY 10025-9992
212–969–0710

Has no national office; check local area for groups or for Shopaholic or Spendthrifter groups.

Drugs Anonymous

Formerly Pill-Anonymous; has no national headquarters. Look for groups in your area.

Gam-Anon

Holds meetings for family members of problem gamblers; check local listings.

Gamblers Anonymous, International Office
PO Box 17173
Los Angeles, CA 90017
213–386–8789

This fellowship of men and women helps solve the common problem of compulsive gambling. There are no dues, fees, or age restrictions.

Incest Survivors Resource Network, International, Inc.
PO Box 911
Hicksville, NY 11802
516–935–3031

Trained incest survivors assist agencies in planning and delivering staff training, workshops or conferences. Provides videotapes and referrals.

Nar-Anon

Holds meetings for family members of people who are involved in drug abuse; check local listings.

Narcotics Anonymous–World Service Office (NA)
PO Box 9999
Van Nuys, CA 91409
818–780–3951

Refers callers to the NA office or groups in their area; free order form for low-cost literature on addiction and how NA works.

National Association of Children of Alcoholics (NACOA)
31582 Coast Highway
South Laguna, CA 92677
714–499–3889

Offers lists of publications, assists in the formation of state chapters, and provides educational and informational material for all ages at no charge. Holds regional conferences and an annual national convention.

National Child Abuse Hotline
Childhelp USA
PO Box 630
Hollywood, CA 90028
800–4–A–CHILD (800–422–4453)

Concerned with the treatment and prevention of child abuse; operates a national twenty-four-hour hotline offering crisis counseling by professionals and referrals to services in your local area; provides literature to parents under stress, for children from age two, and for the professional practitioner. Fees are charged for some literature; others are free.

National Committee for Prevention of Child Abuse
332 South Michigan Avenue
Suite 950
Chicago, IL 60604
312–663–3520

Offers a free packet of general information on the issue of child abuse.

National Council on Alcoholism (NCA)
12 West 21st Street
8th Floor
New York, NY 10010
212–206–6770

Refers callers to its affiliates across the country; free catalog of many publications that can be purchased.

National Council on Compulsive Gambling, Inc.
445 West 59th Street
New York, NY 10019
212–765–3833

Disseminates information and educational materials on gambling as a psychological addiction; refers to treatment facilities and to Twelve-Step groups. Literature is free; *Journal of Gambling Behavior* (a quarterly) is $34.00 per year to individuals and $88.00 to institutions.

National Institute of Drug Abuse (NIDA)
Parklawn Building, 5600 Fishers Lane
Rockville, MD 20852

Information Office: 301–443–6245
For help: 800–662–HELP (800–662–4357)

Day and evening hotline offering referrals to treatment centers, Twelve-Step groups, and general information on drugs. Free pamphlets.

For employers: 800–843–4971

Informational hotline, 9 A.M. to 8 P.M., for employers who are concerned about the drug intake and drug testing of employees.

For literature:
National Clearinghouse for Information
PO Box 416
Kensington, MD 20895

Write for free catalog.

National Self-Help Clearinghouse
33 West 42nd Street
New York, NY 10036
212–642–2944

Refers callers to the clearinghouse resource in their area; offers the *Self-Help Reporter* for $10.00 per year and a booklet, *How to Start a Self-Help Group*, for $6.00.

O-Anon

Holds meetings for family members of people with certain eating disorders; check local listings.

Overeaters Anonymous–National Office
4025 Spence Street
Suite 203
Torrance, CA 90503
213–542–8363

Refers callers to meetings in their area; free introductory literature.

Parents Anonymous—National Office
6733 South Sepulveda Boulevard
Suite 270
Los Angeles, CA 90045
800–421–0353

Telephone crisis counseling, referral to services in local area, and literature free to parents ($5.00 to others).

Sex Addicts Anonymous
PO Box 3038
Minneapolis, MN 55403
612–339–0217

This is a fellowship of men and women who share their experiences, strengths, and hope with each other so they may overcome their sexual addictions or dependencies.

Sexaholics Anonymous
PO Box 300
Simi Valley, CA 93062
805–339–0217

This is a twelve step program patterned after Alcoholics Anonymous for people with a sexual addiction.

BIBLIOGRAPHY

Al-Anon Family Group Headquarters. *A Guide for the Family of the Alcoholic*. New York, undated.

———. *Living with Sobriety*. New York; 1987.

Alcoholics Anonymous World Services. *Alcoholics Anonymous*. New York, 1976.

Anonymous [Julia H.] *Letting Go with Love*. Los Angeles: Jeremy P. Tarcher, 1987.

Anonymous [Dr. Earle M.] *Physician: Heal Thyself*. Minneapolis, Minn.: CompCare, 1989.

Anonymous [Rachel V.] *Family Secrets: Life Stories of ACOAs*. San Francisco: Harper & Row, 1987.

Beattie, Melody. *Co-Dependent No More*. Minneapolis, Minn.: Hazelden, 1987.

Beck, Aaron, T., MD. *Love Is Never Enough*. New York: Harper & Row, 1988.

Bepko, Claudia, and JoAnn Krestan. *The Responsibility Trap: A Blueprint for Treating the Alcoholic Family*. New York: Free Press, 1985.

Black, Claudia. *It Will Never Happen to Me!* Denver, Colo.: MAC Publishing Co., 1981.

Campbell, Susan M. *The Couple's Journey*. San Luis Obispo, Calif.: Impact Publishers, 1986.

Casey, Karen. *If Only I Could Quit.* Minneapolis, Minn.: Hazelden, 1987.

Cermack, Timmen L., MD. *Diagnosing and Treating Co-Dependence.* Minneapolis, Minn.: Johnson Institute Books, 1986.

———. *A Time to Heal.* Los Angeles: Jeremy P. Tarcher, 1989.

Crewson, John. *By Silence Betrayed.* Boston: Little Brown & Co., 1988.

Davis, Donald I., MD. *Alcoholism Treatment: An Integrative Family and Individual Approach.* New York: Gardner Press, 1987.

Diamond, Jed. *Looking for Love in All the Wrong Places.* New York: G. P. Putnam's Sons, 1988.

Dulfano, Celia. *Families, Alcoholism and Recovery: Ten Stories.* Minneapolis, Minn.: Hazelden, 1982.

Earle, Ralph, and Gregory Craw. *Lonely All the Time: Recognizing, Understanding and Overcoming Sex Addiction.* New York: Simon & Schuster, 1989.

Elkin, Michael. *Families Under the Influence.* New York: W. W. Norton & Co., 1984.

Fields, Nina S. *The Well-Seasoned Marriage.* New York: Gardner Press, 1986.

Forward, Susan. *Toxic Parents.* New York: Bantam Books, 1989.

Fossum, Merle, and Marilyn Mason. *Facing Shame: Families in Recovery.* New York: W. W. Norton & Co., 1986.

Friel, John, and Linda Friel. *Adult Children: The Secrets of Dysfunctional Families.* Pompano Beach, Fla.: Health Communications, 1988.

Helmering, Doris Wild. *Happily Ever After.* New York: Warner Books, 1986.

Hodgson, Harriet W. *Parents Recover Too: When Your Child Comes Home From Treatment.* Minneapolis, Minn.: Hazelden, 1988.

Kano, Susan. *Making Peace with Food.* New York: Harper & Row, 1989.

Kellerman, Joseph L. *Grief: A Basic Reaction to Alcoholism.* Minneapolis, Minn.: Hazelden, 1977.

L'Abate, Luciano, et al. *Methods of Family Therapy.* Englewood Cliffs, N.J.: Prentice-Hall, 1986.

Larsen, Earnie. *Stage II Recovery: Life Beyond Addiction.* San Francisco: Harper & Row, 1985.

Lerner, Harriet Goldhor. *The Dance of Intimacy.* New York: Harper & Row, 1989.

Maxwell, Ruth. *Breakthrough: What to Do When Alcoholism or Chemical Dependency Hits Close to Home*. New York: Ballantine Books, 1986.

Miller, Merlene, and Terence T. Gorski. *Family Recovery: Growing Beyond Addiction*. Missouri: Independence Press, 1982.

Miller, Sheron, Daniel Wackman, Elan Nunnally, and Carol Saline. *Straight Talk*. New York: New American Library, 1982.

Mumey, Jack. *Loving an Alcoholic: Help and Hope for Co-Dependents*. New York: Bantam Books, 1988.

Napier, Augustus Y. *The Fragile Bond*. New York: Harper & Row, 1988.

O'Gormon, Patricia, and Philip Oliver-Diaz. *Breaking the Cycle of Addiction*. Pompano Beach, Fla.: Health Communications, 1987.

Orange, Cynthia. *Feeling Left Out?* Minneapolis, Minn.: Hazelden, 1987.

Paul, Jordan, and Margaret Paul. *Do I Have to Give Up Me to Be Loved by You?* Minneapolis, Minn.: CompCare, 1983.

Pittman, Frank S. III, MD. *Turning Points*. New York: W. W. Norton & Co., 1987.

Porterfield, Kay Marie. *Keeping Promises: The Challenge of the Sober Parent*. Minneapolis, Minn.: Hazelden, 1984.

Reddy, Betty. *Alcoholism—A Family Illness*. Park Ridge, Ill.: Lutheran Center for Substance Abuse, 1977.

Reddy, Betty, and Orville McElfresh. *Detachment: Recovery for Family Members*. Park Ridge, Ill.: Parkside Medical Services Corp. 1987.

Rubin, Lillian B. *Just Friends*. New York: Perennial Library, Harper & Row, 1985.

Satir, Virginia. *The New Peoplemaking*. Mountain View, Calif.: Science & Behavior Books, 1988.

Scarf, Maggie. *Intimate Partners*. New York: Random House, 1987.

Schaeff, A. W. *Co-Dependency: Misunderstood—Mistreated*. New York: Harper & Row, 1986.

Schneider, Jennifer P., MD. *Back from Betrayal*. San Francisco: Harper & Row, 1988.

Siegel, Michele, Judith Brisman, and Margot Weinshel. *Surviving an Eating Disorder*. New York: Harper & Row, 1988.

Smith, Ann W. *Grandchildren of Alcoholics*. Pompano Beach, Fla.: Health Communications, 1988.

Smith, Cynthia S. *The Seven Levels of Marriage*. New York: Ivy Books, 1986.

Strayhorn, Joseph M., Jr. *Talking It Out: A Guide to Effective Communication and Problem Solving*. Champaign, Ill.: Research Press, 1977.

Wallace, John. *Alcoholism: New Light on the Disease*. Newport, R.I.: Edgehill Publications, 1985.

Wegscheider-Cruse, Sharon. *Another Chance: Hope and Health for the Alcoholic Family*. Palo Alto, Calif.: Science & Behavior Books, 1980.

Wegscheider-Cruse, Sharon. *Coupleship*. Pompano Beach, Fla.: Health Communications, 1988.

Woititz, Janet Geringer. *Struggle for Intimacy*. Pompano Beach, Fla.: Health Communications, 1985.

Zimberg, Sheldon, John Wallace, and Sheila B. Blume. *Practical Approaches to Alcoholism Psychotherapy*, 2nd ed. New York: Plenum Press, 1985.

INDEX